Essential Questions Journal

Pearson
ECONOMICS

PEARSON

Upper Saddle River, New Jersey   Boston, Massachusetts   Chandler, Arizona   Glenview, Illinois

Pearson ® is a trademark, in the U.S. and/or in other countries, of Pearson plc or its affiliates.
Prentice Hall ® is a trademark, in the U.S. and/or in other countries, of Pearson Education, Inc., or its affiliates.

ISBN 10: 0-13-368039-8
ISBN 13: 978-0-13-368039-3
1 2 3 4 5 6 7 8 9 10 12 11 10 09 08

Table of Contents

Table of Contents

How to Use This Book

The **Essential Questions Journal** will help you to better understand economic principles using real-world applications. Use this journal to develop the framework of your responses to the Essential Questions found in *Economics* and *Foundations Series: Economics*. As you build your understanding and answer the Chapter Essential Questions, you will be beginning to shape your response to the overarching Unit Essential Questions.

The **Unit Essential Question** helps you to think about the ways in which economic principles shape your world.

The **Chapter Essential Question** addresses the main idea of each chapter and contributes to the answer you are forming for the Unit Essential Question.

The Unit and Chapter Warmups help you to begin thinking about the important ideas and Essential Questions of each unit and chapter. They tap into what you already know and set you on a path to learning more.

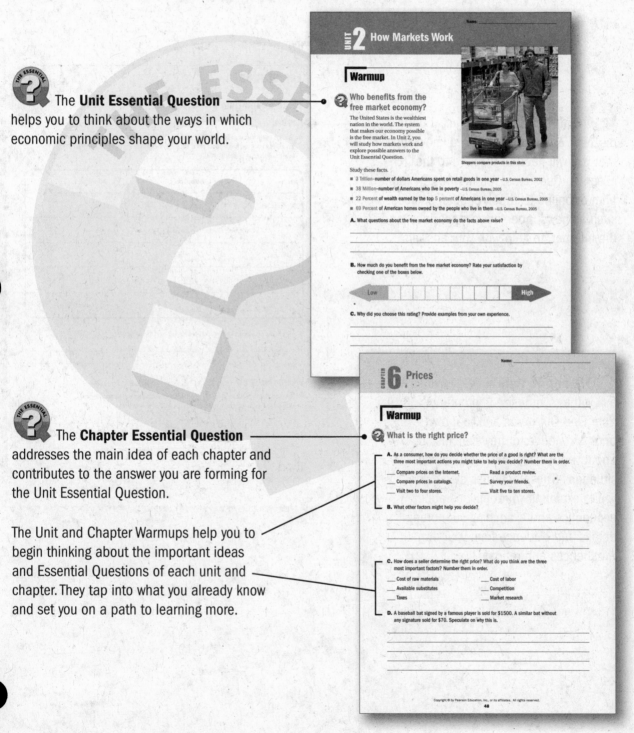

How to Use This Book

The engaging questions and activities in the **Chapter Explorations** challenge you to think creatively and use what you learn about the main ideas and economic terms of the chapter. They will also help you to form your responses to the Chapter and Unit Essential Questions.

Find Out activities direct you to discover, organize, and record knowledge that you will need to respond to the Essential Questions. You may review your print or online textbook or other sources, such as newspaper, news magazines, and the Internet, to help with your answers.

What Do You Think? activities ask you to synthesize information from Find Out items and your own prior knowledge to draw conclusions about various economic issues and situations. These activities also guide you in exploring your opinions about economics and examining supporting details and evidence from your own experiences and reading.

CHAPTER 6 What is the right price?   Name: _____

Exploration

I. Price Equilibrium and Disequilibrium

Find Out

A. Price is not static. It goes up or down under different conditions. Complete the chart by explaining what you know about price, supply, and demand in each situation. The first row has been completed for you.

Price	Supply	Demand
Equilibrium	Equal	Equal
	High supply; surplus	
Low price		
Price floor		
		High demand

B. Why might an economist think that price floors hurt the economy?

_____

_____

What Do You Think?

C. The National Organ Transplant Act of 1984 prohibits the sale of human organs. Why do you think the government forbids the sale of human organs?

_____

_____

_____

The **Chapter Essential Question Activity** pages allow you to experience real-life perspectives on the chapter Essential Questions. The **Chapter Essay** page provides you with various perspectives related to the Chapter Essential Question. These pages will help you synthesize your ideas for responding to the Chapter Essential Question and for writing your Chapter Essay.

The **Chapter Essential Question Activity** gives you the information you need to complete the Essential Question Activity in your textbook. This activity will help you extend your economic thinking and draw conclusions about the Chapter Essential Question.

You can complete the **Chapter Essential Question Activity** using the worksheet provided in your Essential Questions Journal or the electronic worksheet available at PearsonSuccessNet.

The **Chapter Essay** begins with quotations, facts, or situations that relate to the Chapter Essential Question. The second part asks for your thoughts on this information, the Guiding Questions in your textbook, and the activities you have completed in your journal and at Economics Online.

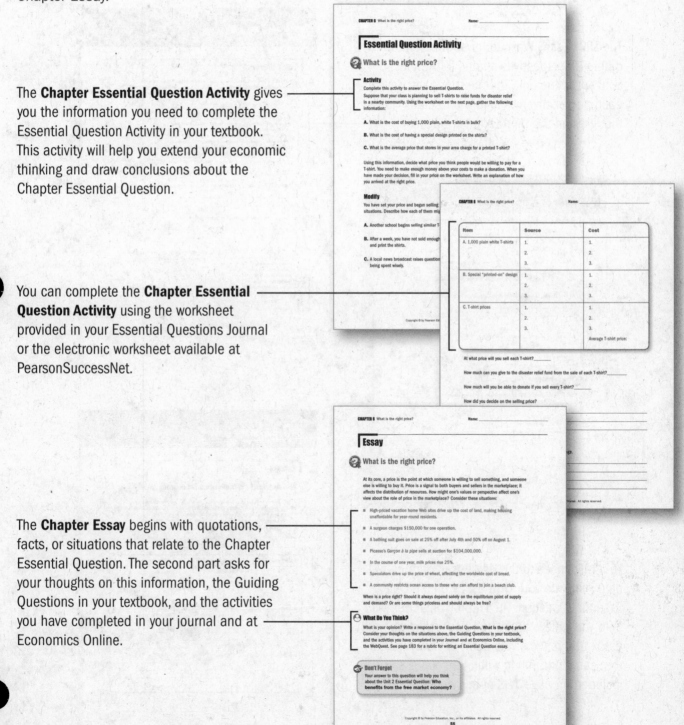

How to Use This Book

The **Unit Essay Warmup** and **Unit Essay** will help you focus your thinking on the Unit Essential Question. The Unit Essay Warmups ask questions about two quotations and a visual related to the main topics of the unit. The Unit Essay page also provides a graphic organizer to help you organize your thoughts about the Unit Essential Question. These pages will also help you be better prepared for exams in school and standardized tests.

The **Unit Essay Warmup** gives you several different perspectives related to the main concept of the unit. The questions that follow each perspective will help you to clarify your thoughts on the Unit Essential Question.

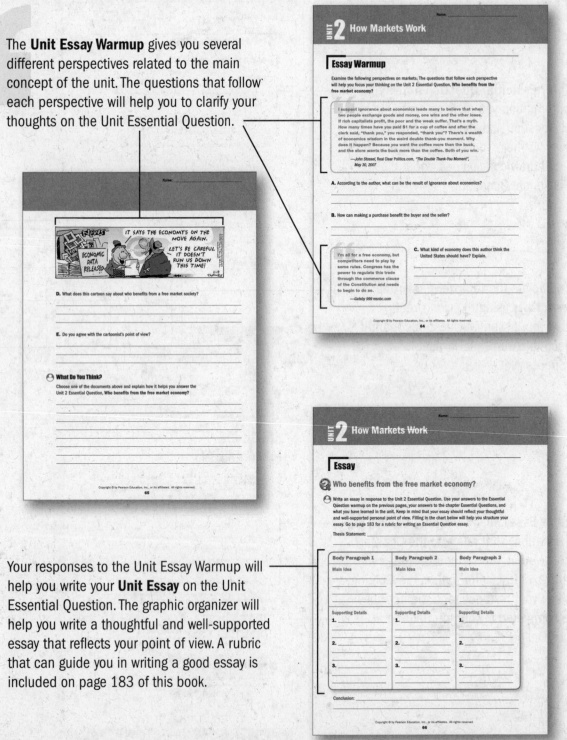

Your responses to the Unit Essay Warmup will help you write your **Unit Essay** on the Unit Essential Question. The graphic organizer will help you write a thoughtful and well-supported essay that reflects your point of view. A rubric that can guide you in writing a good essay is included on page 183 of this book.

Unit 1

Introduction to Economics

 Essential Question

How does economics affect everyone?

Chapter 1 Essential Question

How can we make the best economic choices?

Chapter 2 Essential Question

How does a society decide who gets what goods and services?

Chapter 3 Essential Question

What role should government play in a free market economy?

UNIT 1 Introduction to Economics

Warmup

How does economics affect everyone?

Although we don't think about it much, economics affects our activities every day. In Unit 1, you will be introduced to the world of economics and explore possible responses to the Unit Essential Question above.

Think about your daily activities, the choices you make, and your dreams. Then, complete the chart.

Building bridges requires making many good decisions, including economic ones. Studying economics helps us all make better decisions.

How does economics affect your choices?	How does economics affect you?
What are your three favorite foods? pizza, ice cream, apples, fresh peas	Economics affects the prices of foods, so it affects how often I eat my favorite foods. It makes fresh foods such as apples and peas more expensive when they're out of season.
What is your favorite class at school?	
What are your two favorite after-school activities or hobbies?	
What are your three favorite books?	
What are your three favorite movies?	
What are three of your future goals?	

CHAPTER 1

What Is Economics?

Warmup

 ## How can we make the best economic choices?

A. Which of the following items are *needs?* Which are *wants?* Classify each one with an **N** or a **W**.

_____ a source of clean water   _____ a healthy lunch   _____ a beach vacation

_____ concert tickets   _____ a safe place to live   _____ a laptop computer

_____ health insurance   _____ a new watch   _____ a winter coat

B. List some of your basic needs. Describe how one is met.

_____

_____

_____

C. List some of your wants. Which one is most important to you? Describe your plan for meeting it.

_____

_____

_____

D. How does scarcity—limited resources—affect how your needs and wants are met?

_____

_____

_____

_____

Exploration

I. Scarcity, Choices, and You

➡ Find Out

A. All resources are scarce, or limited, including time, money, and land. Scarcity forces us to make choices about our resources. This simple fact is the basis of economics. Explore scarcity and choices by completing the chart below.

	What is the resource?	**Why is the resource scarce?**	**What are some options for using the resource?**
Your grandmother gives you $25 for your birthday.	money		
Your school closes two hours early today.			watch TV, study, work at a job
A reservoir supplies your community with water.		Sources of water are limited.	
Your state government collects sales taxes.			

👤 What Do You Think?

B. Based on your own thinking, rank the following resources in the United States from 1 (most important) to 10 (least important):

☐ oil   ☐ health care   ☐ drinking water   ☐ job programs for teens

☐ national security   ☐ libraries   ☐ farmland   ☐ college scholarships

☐ Internet access   ☐ wind turbines

Explain the reasons for your #1 resource ranking and your #10 resource ranking.

_____

_____

C. Consider something that is scarce in your life. Identify what it is and why it is scarce. Then explain what options you have for increasing it or using it more efficiently.

_____

_____

Name: _____

II. Needed: Land, Labor, Capital

→ Find Out

A. Production of a good or a service requires land (natural resources), labor, and capital (physical capital and human capital). Suppose that you are an entrepreneur. List at least one example of each factor of production you would need to start up the following new businesses:

New Wave Hair Salon

Land (resources)	Labor hair stylists
Physical capital	Human capital training in hair care

Organic Foods Diner

Land (resources) supply of organic vegetables	Labor
Physical capital oven	Human capital

👤 What Do You Think?

B. Suppose that one of the businesses above is not doing as well as you expected after being open for a full year. What changes in the factors of production could you make to improve productivity?

_____

_____

_____

_____

III. What's the Trade-Off?

➔ Find Out

A. Every choice we make involves trade-offs. The most valuable option that we did not choose is the opportunity cost. What are the trade-offs for each situation below? What is the opportunity cost for each, and why?

Example: You buy a personal music system for $50.	A business spends $10,000 on advertising.	The U.S. government spends $10 million for extra security at airports.
Trade-offs: - not adding to college savings - not buying a new video game - not buying new clothes	Trade-offs:	Trade-offs:
Opportunity Cost: Because you plan to go to college next year, your opportunity cost is not adding to college savings.	Opportunity Cost:	Opportunity Cost:

● What Do You Think?

B. Compare the marginal costs and the marginal benefits in the chart below. Then answer the question that follows.

Decision Making Grid

Options	Marginal Benefit	Marginal Cost
1. Practice guitar 2 more hours per week	Learn 2 new songs	One lawn mowing job, which would pay $15
2. Practice guitar 3 more hours per week	Learn 3 new songs	2 lawn mowing jobs, which would pay $30
3. Practice guitar 4 more hours per week	Learn 4 new songs	2 lawn mowing jobs, which would pay $30

Since the marginal cost for options 2 and 3 are the same, which option would you choose? Explain.

_____

_____

_____

IV. What and How Much to Produce?

➔ Find Out

A. Your older cousin is considering selling home-baked cakes and cookies. However, your cousin has just one oven to use, and the cookies and cakes each bake at different temperatures and for different amounts of time. How can your cousin make the most efficient use of one oven? Plot your cousin's production possibilities curve, using the numbers in the table below.

Cakes	Batches of Cookies
0	30
2	29
5	26
9	20
11	12
12	0

Title: _____

Cakes

Label: _____

B. How can your cousin improve production? How can your cousin avoid underutilization (that is, reducing production)? Mark each of the following items with an **R** if it will improve production (shifting the curve to the right) or an **L** if it will hurt production (shifting the curve to the left).

_____ a bigger oven   _____ a new recipe reduces baking time

_____ hires an assistant   _____ a shortage of flour

👤 What Do You Think?

C. Suppose that your cousin decides to significantly increase the production of cakes one day. You worry that your cousin is ignoring the law of increasing costs. What would you advise your cousin to do first, and why?

_____

_____

D. Select one business that interests you (for example, a local restaurant). Describe some possible investments in physical capital and in human capital that could improve production possibilities for that business.

_____

_____

Essential Question Activity

 ## How can we make the best economic choices?

Activity

Complete this activity to answer the Essential Question.

As you have learned, scarcity and opportunity cost lie at the heart of all economic decisions—including those you make. You have limited time and limited resources. Every time you choose one alternative, you give up something else. Using the worksheet on the next page, keep track of how you use your resources for the next three days.

A. In Column 1, record at least three items on which you spent your money and three activities on which you spent your time.

B. In Column 2, list the opportunity cost for each entry in Column 1. Remember that the opportunity cost is the next most desirable alternative—the thing you gave up when you made your choice.

After completing the chart, review your choices. Then, for each of the choices, you made, answer the following questions:

If you had it to do over again, would you make the same choice? Why or why not?

Write your answers in Column 3.

Modify

You have listed your choices and trade-offs and evaluated your outcomes. Now consider how your choices might have differed if your resources had differed. Write an answer to each of the following.

A. How would your choices change if you had 10 percent more money to spend?

B. What would you give up if you had five fewer hours of free time to use in those three days?

C. Pick one of the opportunity costs on your list. What conditions might have led you to make the opposite choice? Explain.

Column 1	Column 2	Column 3
Things you spent money on Example: $5 on an ice-cream sundae ■ _____ _____ _____ ■ _____ _____ _____ ■ _____ _____ _____	**Opportunity cost—what you gave up** Example: 2 slices of pizza ■ _____ _____ _____ ■ _____ _____ _____ ■ _____ _____ _____	**Would you make the same choice again? Why or why not?** Example: Yes, because . . . ■ _____ _____ _____ ■ _____ _____ _____ ■ _____ _____ _____
Things you spent time on ■ _____ _____ _____ ■ _____ _____ _____ ■ _____ _____ _____	**Opportunity cost—what you gave up** ■ _____ _____ _____ ■ _____ _____ _____ ■ _____ _____ _____	**Would you make the same choice again? Why or why not?** ■ _____ _____ _____ ■ _____ _____ _____ ■ _____ _____ _____

Modify

Respond to situation A or B, given on the previous page.

_____

_____

Respond to situation C, given on the previous page.

_____

_____

Essay

How can we make the best economic choices?

Because resources are limited, everyone needs to make choices about how they are used. Economics studies how individuals, businesses, and governments make those choices. Making the best economic choices can be complicated. Consider the following choices.

- A student needs to decide whether to get a job after school, take part in an after-school activity, or study longer to get better grades.

- A teacher is deciding if class on Friday would be best spent by giving a lecture, directing small group discussions, or having students do independent research.

- A homeowner is figuring out whether to invest in a new lawnmower, new steps for the back porch, or paint for the house.

- A business owner needs to decide about investing more money for new computers, new delivery trucks, or more employee training.

- A town government is sorting out whether to increase the school budget, hire more firefighters, or make improvements in public parks.

- The U.S. government needs to decide if it should keep a national wildlife area closed to all development, limit development to one area, or allow some development in all areas.

What Do You Think?

What is your opinion? Write a response to the Essential Question, **How can we make the best economic choices?** Consider the topics above, the Guiding Questions in your textbook, and the activities you have completed in your Journal and at Economics Online, including the WebQuest. See page 183 for a rubric for writing an Essential Question essay.

Don't Forget

Your answer to this question will help you think about the Unit 1 Essential Question: **How does economics affect everyone?**

CHAPTER 2 Economic Systems

Warmup

 How does a society decide who gets what goods and services?

Suppose that a country with 10 million people could produce 21 million pairs of shoes in a year. There are many ways to divide up the shoes among the people.

👤👤👤👤👤👤👤👤 👟👟👟👟👟👟👟👟👟👟👟👟👟	👤👤👤👤👤👤 👟👟👟👟👟👟👟👟👟👟👟👟👟👟👟	👤 👟👟👟👟👟
👤👤 👟👟👟👟👟👟	👤👤👤👤 👟👟👟👟	👤 👟👟👟
		👤👤👤👤👤👤👤👤 👟👟👟👟👟👟👟👟👟👟👟👟👟👟 👤

👤 = 1 million people   👟 = 1 million pairs of shoes

A. Circle the distribution that seems the best to you. Explain your choice.

_____

_____

B. If you were the one who got five pairs of shoes, would your opinion change? Why or why not?

_____

_____

C. If you were the one who got no shoes, would your opinion change? Why or why not?

_____

_____

D. Should a country control how goods and services are distributed? Explain.

_____

_____

CHAPTER 2 How does a society decide who gets what goods and services?

Name: _____

Exploration

I. Analyzing a Society's Economic Goals and Values

➡ Find Out

A. Societies must answer the three key economic questions: What to produce? How to produce it? Who consumes it? Sometimes societies answer these questions without fully analyzing which goals and values are most important to them. Match the choices in Column 1 with the goals and values they best support in Column 2.

Column 1 Choices	Column 2 Goals and Values
1. Every citizen is required to work at a government job. The difference in worker pay rates is very small.	____ Economic efficiency
2. A country guarantees that every person will receive adequate food, shelter, and clothing.	____ Economic freedom
3. A country chooses to grow coffee instead of corn. Most of its farmland is mountainous and best suited for coffee.	____ Economic security
4. The government offers tax breaks for companies that develop and use new technologies.	____ Economic equity
5. A worker chooses to change jobs every few years, but sometimes ends up unemployed.	____ Economic growth

👤 What Do You Think?

B. Both the United States and Canada have decided to produce high-quality health care for their citizens. However, how they pay for (that is, produce) health care differs.

U.S. Health Care System	Canadian Health Care System
Most care is paid by individuals/companies, using private insurance.	Most care is paid by taxes.

Which societal goals and values listed in Column 2 (top chart) are reflected in the U.S. health care system? In the Canadian system? Provide support for your response.

_____

_____

_____

_____

Name: _____

II. A Look at Free Markets

→ Find Out

A. A husband works for a computer manufacturer and his wife works for a law firm. Both are paid a salary. They decide to buy a new car when their first child is born. Identify the three firms in the example and what they are buying in the factor market and selling in the product market. Also, identify the household and describe what it is selling in the factor market and what it is buying in the product market.

Firm	Buying in factor market	Selling in product market
Law firm	Wife's labor	

Household	Selling in factor market	Buying in product market

👤 What Do You Think?

B. Free markets depend on voluntary exchanges. Suppose that you are looking for a birthday present for your mother who likes to work around the home. You have $20 to spend and want to buy her a hammer. Which choice would you make?

 average quality
brand name hammer
$20

 ?

 average quality
store brand hammer
$16

 high quality hammer
$30

average quality
nail gun
$100

Circle your choice, and then explain how it reflects self-interest.

_____

_____

C. If other buyers made the same choice as you, how might it affect the firms that offer hammers or nail guns? Explain how these choices illustrate customer sovereignty.

_____

_____

CHAPTER 2 How does a society decide who gets what goods and services?

Name: _____

III. A Look at Centrally Planned Economies

➡ Find Out

A. Fill in the descriptions of how decisions are made in a free market economy and a centrally planned economy.

Free Market Economy	**Centrally Planned Economy**
Individuals and firms decide what and how much to produce.	Government decides what and how much to produce.
How are prices set?	How are prices set?
How is labor supplied and wages set?	How is labor supplied and wages set?
What are the effects on consumers?	What are the effects on consumers?

👤 What Do You Think?

B. At one time, the centrally planned economy of China encouraged farmers to produce iron in their backyards, rather than have factories make iron. This proved unsuccessful, since most of the farmers' iron was of poor quality. Why do you think this approach was unsuccessful? How could this experiment become a success in a free market economy?

_____

_____

_____

C. In theory, centrally planned economies allow all people to consume goods equally. In reality, however, people at upper levels are paid more and have access to more goods. Why do you think this has been true?

_____

_____

_____

CHAPTER 2 How does a society decide who gets what goods and services?

Name: _____

IV. A Look at Mixed Economies

➡ Find Out

A. Fill in one example of how a government might need to be involved in a mixed economy for each listed government role.

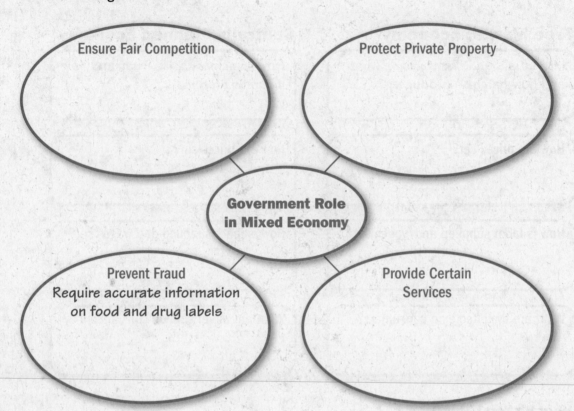

Ensure Fair Competition

Protect Private Property

Government Role in Mixed Economy

Prevent Fraud
Require accurate information on food and drug labels

Provide Certain Services

👤 What Do You Think?

In mixed economies, the government plays a key role in both the factor market and the product market.

B. What do you think is the proper role of government in the factor market, and why?

_____

_____

_____

C. What do you think is the proper role of government in the product market, and why?

_____

_____

_____

CHAPTER 2 How does a society decide who gets what goods and services?

Name: _____

V. Comparing Mixed Economies

→ Find Out

A. Analyze the economies of the hypothetical countries below. How does each one rate in terms of its government involvement in its economy? Place the number of each country in the appropriate box on the "Government in Economy" scale. Note that the United States is placed near to a pure free market economy.

Country #1	Country #2	Country #3	Country #4
It does not regulate banking or place any restrictions on foreign investment.	It owns and controls public transportation and natural resources such as mines, forests, and oil wells.	It owns all businesses and resources, except family farms.	It does not own any businesses, but controls prices for all resources.

Government in Economy

Centrally Planned ← [ ] [ ] [ ] [ ] [ ] [ ] [ ] U.S.A. [ ] [ ] → **Free Market**

B. Choose one of the hypothetical countries above and explain why you rated it as you did.

_____

_____

_____

_____

👤 What Do You Think?

C. Many European governments require companies to give their workers four weeks or more of paid vacation each year. How do you think this might affect their economies? Why do you think the United States does not require companies to offer paid vacations?

_____

_____

_____

_____

CHAPTER 2 How does a society decide who gets what goods and services?

Name: _____

Essential Question Activity

 How does a society decide who gets what goods and services?

Activity

Complete this activity to answer the Essential Question.

Imagine that your class is advising leaders of the newly-formed nation, Ervola. Many of the nation's new political leaders favor the use of central planning, but business leaders favor a laissez-faire approach. Ervola must determine which economic system will help it meet the economic goals stated in Section 1 of this chapter.

Use the format of a debate and the worksheet on the next page to help your team prepare. Before the debate, participants should identify the economic goals and determine how their team plans to meet each of them. (Participants should decide on the rules of the debate in advance.)

A. For the affirmative, a student team will develop arguments in favor of a strict command economy.

B. For the negative, another student team will develop arguments in favor of a totally free market economy.

Modify

A. As a class, discuss and evaluate the arguments given in the debate. Base your evaluation on:

■ the logic of the arguments

■ the analysis the speakers used

■ the evidence given

■ the organization of the speeches

■ the persuasiveness of the arguments

B. Present an agreed-upon economic system to recommend to the nation of Ervola. Include the statements that most strongly support your recommendation.

CHAPTER 2 How does a society decide who gets what goods and services?

Name: _____

Position (Circle one.):
Affirmative (supports command economy)
Negative (supports free market)

Societal Goal/Value	How Chosen Economy Helps Meet Goal
Economic efficiency	
Economic freedom	Negative: A free market offers workers and businesses free choices; a command economy does not.
Economic security	Affirmative: A command economy ensures basic employment and access to goods; a free market economy does not.
Economic equity	
Economic growth	

Modify

A. Evaluate the arguments.

_____

_____

B. Explain your recommendation, including the statements of strongest support for your position.

_____

_____

CHAPTER 2 How does a society decide who gets what goods and services?

Name: _____

Essay

How does a society decide who gets what goods and services?

Each society decides what goods to produce, how they get produced, and who gets to consume them. These choices may not always be stated clearly by a government or society, but their choices are revealed by how the economy works. Nearly every economy in the world today is a mixed economy. Different levels of government involvement produce different results. Consider the following generalizations:

- Traditional economies usually promote economic equity. However, because they have little flexibility, they tend to produce little economic security or economic growth.

- A free market economy provides workers with the freedom to choose where they want to work, but those workers may suffer from periods of unemployment.

- A command economy promises full employment, but workers have few incentives to produce more or to suggest innovations that could result in economic growth.

- In theory, command economies create economic equity, since differences in pay for different jobs are very small. Historically, however, there has always been an upper class that received higher pay and had greater access to more goods.

- Free market economies usually produce a large selection of consumer goods and services at varying prices. Goods and services, however, are often distributed unevenly because of greater differences in incomes between the rich and the poor.

- Mixed economies must constantly make decisions to select one goal over another. For example, unemployment benefits may result in less economic growth because of higher taxes, but more economic security.

What Do You Think?

What is your opinion? Write a response to the Essential Question, **How does a society decide who gets what goods and services?** Consider the generalizations above, the Guiding Questions in your textbook, and the activities you have completed in your Journal and at Economics Online, including the WebQuest. See page 183 for a rubric for writing an Essential Question essay.

 Don't Forget
Your answer to this question will help you think about the Unit 1 Essential Question: **How does economics affect everyone?**

CHAPTER 3 — American Free Enterprise

Warmup

? What role should government play in a free market economy?

Choose the response below that best reflects how you would want government to act in each situation.

A. After a law changes, many banks make risky investments and lose billions of dollars. The banks may go out of business, resulting in many investors losing their money.

___ take no action

___ help both the banks and the investors

___ help the investors only

___ help the banks only

B. A company develops a new drug, which it sells to help people lose weight. It works well for most people, but for some it causes stomach problems.

___ take no action

___ remove the drug from the market

___ let the drug still be sold, but with a warning

___ require more testing before deciding if the drug can be sold again

C. Several families are building houses on a mountain near a large town. The road to these houses is very narrow, with many curves, and there are frequent car crashes.

___ take no action

___ build a new road, using town taxes

___ require the families to pay for a new road

___ build a new road, but divide costs between the town and the families

D. Review your answers above, and then summarize what role you think government should play in economic issues.

_____

_____

_____

_____

CHAPTER 3 What role should government play in a free market economy?

Name: _____

Exploration

I. Free Enterprise and Government

⮕ Find Out

A. The economic freedoms of Americans are protected by the U.S. Constitution. For each freedom listed below, give one example of how our government protects that freedom and explain the importance of that freedom to our free enterprise system today.

	How does our government protect this freedom?	Why is this freedom important to our free enterprise system today?
Private Property	The Fifth Amendment states that . . .	This freedom allows people to make their own decisions about . . .
Open Opportunity		
Profit Motive		
Legal Equality		
Free Contract		
Voluntary Exchange		

👤 What Do You Think?

B. Besides protecting our economic freedoms, the government also takes actions in the public interest. For example, federal agencies regulate certain industries to protect public health and safety. Choose one of the federal agencies listed in your textbook. Do you think this agency benefits our country? Why or why not?

_____

_____

_____

CHAPTER 3 What role should government play in a free market economy?

Name: _____

II. Governing for Growth and Stability

What Do You Think?

A. Look at the progression of events below. What kind of action, if any, do you think the government should take at each step, and why?

> Consumers worry about higher prices.

↓

> Consumers buy fewer goods.

↓

> Businesses produce fewer goods and lay off workers.

↓

> Consumers have less income and buy fewer goods.

↓

> Some businesses close down.

B. Suppose that it took you two years to invent a device that let light bulbs use two-thirds less energy. You plan to sell your invention to a big company. If the government did not provide patent protection, what might happen to your invention? Explain.

_____

_____

_____

C. In your opinion, which plays a larger role in our country's economic success: government incentives or the American work ethic? Why?

_____

_____

_____

CHAPTER 3 What role should government play in a free market economy?

Name: _____

III. The Costs and Benefits of Public Goods

→ Find Out

A. The NASA budget for 2009 was $17.6 billion, less than one penny for each $1 the federal government spent. However, is the cost for NASA too high compared to the benefits? Complete the chart to identify NASA's costs and benefits. (You can find some of the benefits resulting from NASA's work at www.nasa.gov.)

Costs of NASA	Benefits of NASA
Taxes: $17.6 billion Opportunity costs:	Medical devices

👤 What Do You Think?

B. Based on your completed chart above, do you think that NASA is worth the costs? Why or why not?

_____

_____

C. Suppose that a company wants to buy land in your town to build a mall. Your town would benefit from the increased tax revenues, but the land is now used for recreation. Would you let the company buy the land? Use the graphic below to help you decide.

Costs/Negative Externalities	Benefits/Positive Externalities
• Loss of recreation land • •	• Increased tax revenues • •

Decision and Reasons

D. Your town needs to raise taxes for its schools. People with no children protest. What do you think? Include references to positive and negative externalities in your answer.

_____

_____

CHAPTER 3 What role should government play in a free market economy?

Name: _____

IV. Stretching Out the Safety Net

➔ Find Out

A. Fill in the chart below using the different redistribution programs discussed in your textbook. Types of programs include cash, in-kind, medical, and education.

Program	Who It Serves	Type of Program	Reasons for This Type of Assistance
Workers Compensation	Workers injured on the job	Cash	Provides income for people who are temporarily/ permanently unable to work

👤 What Do You Think?

B. The goals of economic freedom, equity, and security discussed in Chapter 2 often come into conflict when governments provide a safety net. Select one of the redistribution programs noted in your completed chart above. Then, describe how it can interfere with economic freedom for some people and how it can promote economic equity and security for others.

_____

_____

_____

_____

C. Review the ways in which government in the United States supports private charity. Then explain what Jeff Schnepper means when he says, "The glory of charitable donations is that you give and receive at the same time."

_____

_____

_____

CHAPTER 3 What role should government play in a free market economy?

Name: _____

Essential Question Activity

 ## What role should government play in a free market economy?

Activity

As a citizen and a consumer, you will always be affected by the role of government in your economic life. Complete this activity to answer the Essential Question, **What role should government play in a free market economy?** For this activity, your class will be divided into four groups. Each group will look in depth at one of the following topics: government regulation; encouraging economic growth; providing public goods; providing an economic safety net.

Research your topic in print or use online news sources that illustrate the government's role. (The section at the bottom of this page lists some reliable sources and keywords you can use in your search.) After your group chooses a story, prepare a brief presentation using the Summary Report Form on the next page. Each group should present its findings and reactions to the whole class.

Modify

After each group has completed its presentation of its findings, the entire class should evaluate the information and discuss the following questions:

A. Was the action taken by the government appropriate to the situation?

B. What other action might the government have taken?

C. What might have happened if the government had taken no action?

D. Based on the particular incident, do you think the government should have more or less influence on the economy?

E. Under what conditions might you feel differently?

Suggested Keywords for Online Searches:

■ Government regulation: startup business; competition; product launch; interest group lobbying (or the names of specific interest or industry groups)

■ Encouraging economic growth: business cycle; expansion; contraction; recession; unemployment rate; regulating financial institutions; new patent; copyright

■ Providing public goods: public goods; public works; pollution controls

■ Providing an economic safety net: TANF; Social Security; Medicare; Medicaid; school funding; education spending; faith-based initiative

Some Reliable Online Sources:

http://usinfo.state.gov; http://www.frbsf.org; http://www.npr.org/

CHAPTER 3 What role should government play in a free market economy?

Name: _____

Summary Report Form

Subject of story (topic):	
Company, industry, group, and/ or government agency involved:	
Action taken (describe briefly):	
Reason for action (What were the goals?):	
Competitive pressures faced (by business) or alternative solutions considered (by government):	
Results (How did the results compare to the reasons for the action?):	
Externalities (positive and negative):	

Modify

Respond to the questions given on the previous page. Use an additional sheet of paper, if necessary.

_____

_____

_____

CHAPTER 3   What role should government play in a free
market economy?

Name: _____

Essay

What role should government play in a free market economy?

In the United States, government is constantly making decisions that affect the local, state, national, and global economies. Citizens, businesses, and elected officials often disagree on the role of government in the economy. Consider these issues:

■ The U.S. Constitution and its amendments protect private property rights, allow the government to collect taxes, and guarantee the right to make contracts. How does our constitution affect our economy?

■ Government regulations help people get accurate information and help protect people's health and safety. Some regulations cost businesses money and can interfere with their economic freedom. What is the correct balance between too much government regulation and not enough?

■ Government provides public goods, such as roads, which could not be efficiently produced by individuals or businesses. Government weighs positive and negative externalities related to public goods. How essential are public goods to our economy?

■ Some people believe that the government plays too great a role in certain areas of our economy, such as health care and the environment. Should the role of government be reduced in some areas of the economy? In all areas? Or, should the role be increased?

■ The federal government provides a safety net for poor people and it encourages private action to help the poor. Should the government spend tax money on safety net services? If so, what types of services should the government provide?

What Do You Think?

What is your opinion? Write a response to the Essential Question, **What role should government play in a free market economy?** Consider the issues above, the Guiding Questions in your textbook, and the activities you have completed in your Journal and at Economics Online, including the WebQuest. See page 183 for a rubric for writing an Essential Question essay.

Don't Forget

Your answer to this question will help you think about the Unit 1 Essential Question: **How does economics affect everyone?**

UNIT 1 Introduction to Economics

Essay Warmup

Examine the following perspectives on the importance of understanding economics. The questions that follow each perspective will help you focus your thinking on the Unit 1 Essential Question, **How does economics affect everyone?**

> Economics is, at root, the study of incentives: how people get what they want, or need, especially when other people want or need the same thing. . . . An incentive is simply a means of urging people to do more of a good thing and less of a bad thing. But most incentives don't come about organically. Someone—an economist or a politician or a parent—has to invent them. Your three-year-old eats all her vegetables for a week? She wins a trip to the toy store. A big steelmaker belches too much smoke into the air? The company is fined for each cubic foot of pollutants over the legal limit.
>
> —*Steven D. Levitt and Stephen J. Dubner,* Freakonomics

A. According to the authors, how are incentives created?

_____

_____

B. What two types of incentives do the authors think are necessary? Provide another example of each.

_____

_____

> Economics surely does not provide a romantic vision of life. But the widespread poverty, misery, and crises in many parts of the world, much of it unnecessary, are strong reminders that understanding economic and social laws can make an enormous contribution to the welfare of people.
>
> —*Gary Becker, Nobel Prize acceptance speech, 1992*

C. How do you think "understanding economic and social laws can make an enormous contribution to the welfare of people"? Provide two or more examples.

_____

_____

"The economy is slowing down. Last night the Tooth Fairy left me an IOU"

D. What does this cartoon suggest about the importance of economics for everyone?

_____

_____

_____

_____

_____

_____

E. Do you agree with this cartoonist's point of view? Why or why not?

_____

_____

_____

What Do You Think?

Choose one of the documents above and explain how it helps you answer the
Unit 1 Essential Question, **How does economics affect everyone?**

_____

_____

_____

_____

_____

_____

_____

_____

_____

_____

_____

UNIT 1 Introduction to Economics

Essay

 How does economics affect everyone?

Write an essay that responds to the Unit 1 Essential Question. Use your answers to the Essential Question warmup on the previous pages, your answers to the chapter Essential Questions, and what you have learned in this unit. Keep in mind that your essay should reflect your thoughtful and well-supported personal point of view. Filling in the chart below will help you structure your essay. Go to page 183 for a rubric for writing an Essential Question essay.

Thesis Statement: _____

_____

Body Paragraph 1	Body Paragraph 2	Body Paragraph 3
Main Idea	**Main Idea**	**Main Idea**
_____ _____ _____ _____	_____ _____ _____ _____	_____ _____ _____ _____
Supporting Details **1.** _____ _____ _____ **2.** _____ _____ _____ **3.** _____ _____ _____	**Supporting Details** **1.** _____ _____ _____ **2.** _____ _____ _____ **3.** _____ _____ _____	**Supporting Details** **1.** _____ _____ _____ **2.** _____ _____ _____ **3.** _____ _____ _____

Conclusion: _____

_____

Unit 2

How Markets Work

 Essential Question

Who benefits from the free market economy?

Chapter 4
Essential Question

How do we decide what to buy?

Chapter 5
Essential Question

How do suppliers decide what goods and services to offer?

Chapter 6
Essential Question

What is the right price?

Chapter 7
Essential Question

How does competition affect your choices?

UNIT 2 How Markets Work

Shoppers compare products in this store.

Warmup

Who benefits from the free market economy?

The United States is the wealthiest nation in the world. The system that makes our economy possible is the free market. In Unit 2, you will study how markets work and explore possible answers to the Unit Essential Question.

Study these facts.

- **3 Trillion-number of dollars Americans spent on retail goods in one year** –U.S. Census Bureau, 2002

- **38 Million-number of Americans who live in poverty** –U.S. Census Bureau, 2005

- **22 Percent of wealth earned by the top 5 percent of Americans in one year** –U.S. Census Bureau, 2005

- **69 Percent of American homes owned by the people who live in them** –U.S. Census Bureau, 2005

A. What questions about the free market economy do the facts above raise?

_____

_____

_____

B. How much do you benefit from the free market economy? Rate your satisfaction by checking one of the boxes below.

Low ☐☐☐☐☐☐☐☐☐☐ High

C. Why did you choose this rating? Provide examples from your own experience.

_____

_____

_____

Warmup

 ## How do we decide what to buy?

A. Consumers have many choices when it comes to buying goods. Read each scenario below. Then, tell what you would do and why.

> Your gas tank is on "E." You have to fill up to get to work. Last week you filled your tank for $30. Today it will cost $50. Would you pay $50 or find alternative transportation?
>
> _____
> _____
> _____
> _____

> The running shoes you want are no longer on sale. The store has discounted a similar pair, but you do not like them. Would you buy the regularly-priced shoes or the discounted pair?
>
> _____
> _____
> _____
> _____

B. Brainstorm a list of goods you would continue to buy, even if they doubled or tripled in price.

_____
_____

C. What factors influence you when buying a particular product? Suppose that you need to buy a pair of jeans to wear to school. Circle three factors from the list below that would affect your purchase the most.

- They are a popular brand at school.
- The company's advertising appeals to you.
- They will cost your entire weekly budget.
- They come with a free T-shirt.

- They are on sale today only.
- There is only one pair left in your size.
- They cost less than other brands.
- There is only one style available.

D. Suppose that you already own three pairs of jeans. Would the factors you circled above change? Would you still buy the jeans? Explain.

_____
_____

Exploration

I. The Law of Demand

→ Find Out

A. The demand for goods and services constantly changes. People buy more or less of something when the price changes. Economists can often predict people's spending patterns. Can you? Complete the sequence charts below by circling the correct answer. One has been done for you.

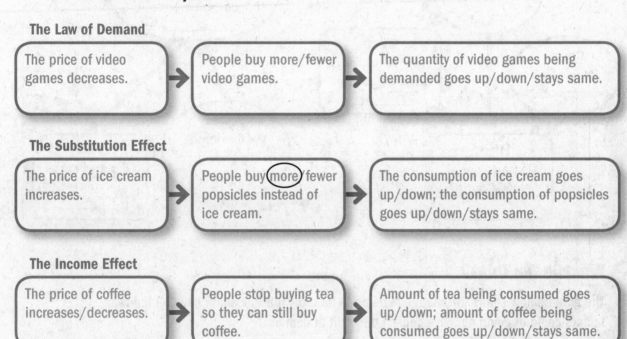

The Law of Demand

| The price of video games decreases. | → | People buy more/fewer video games. | → | The quantity of video games being demanded goes up/down/stays same. |

The Substitution Effect

| The price of ice cream increases. | → | People buy (more)/fewer popsicles instead of ice cream. | → | The consumption of ice cream goes up/down; the consumption of popsicles goes up/down/stays same. |

The Income Effect

| The price of coffee increases/decreases. | → | People stop buying tea so they can still buy coffee. | → | Amount of tea being consumed goes up/down; amount of coffee being consumed goes up/down/stays same. |

B. Suppose that a newer version of your laptop computer has just been released. You want to upgrade your computer, but you can't afford to buy the new model for another two months. How does your situation affect the demand for new laptops.

_____

_____

_____

👤 What Do You Think?

C. How do you think store owners know how much of a good to stock on their shelves?

_____

_____

Name: _____

II. Changes in Demand

➜ Find Out

A. The law of demand is accurate when price is the only condition that changes. However, what happens to demand when other factors change? Fill in the factors that would make the cause-effect charts true.

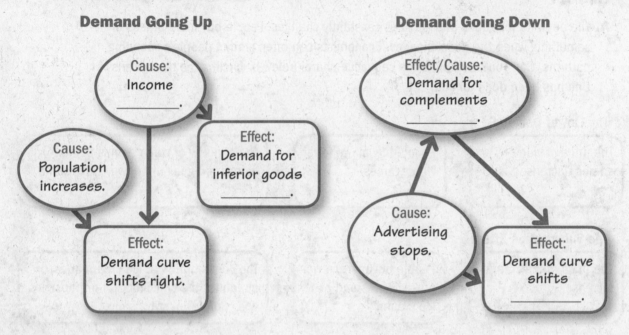

Demand Going Up

Cause: Income _____.

Cause: Population increases.

Effect: Demand for inferior goods _____.

Effect: Demand curve shifts right.

Demand Going Down

Effect/Cause: Demand for complements _____.

Cause: Advertising stops.

Effect: Demand curve shifts _____.

👤 What Do You Think?

The graph below shows the change in demand for a toy robot. Explain how the following factors could or could not have caused this shift in demand.

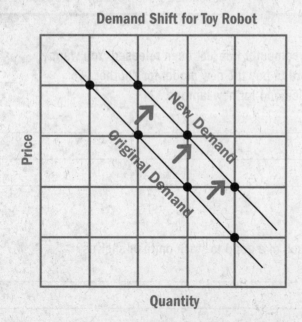

Demand Shift for Toy Robot

Price

New Demand

Original Demand

Quantity

B. A TV advertising campaign for the toy robot targets children ages 6 to 11. The commercials air on Saturday mornings and weekday afternoons.

_____

_____

_____

C. An animated film featuring the toy robot flops at the box office.

_____

_____

_____

III. Elasticity of Demand

➔ Find Out

A. What people buy often depends on a product's elasticity at a given price. Write factors in the boxes below that affect the elasticity of goods. Include examples or a definition for each factor. The first one has been done for you.

Necessities vs. Luxuries
Necessities: car insurance, school supplies, fresh fruit
Luxuries: music downloads, magazines, sports drinks

Elasticity

B. Why would a business owner need to know the elasticity of a product his or her company sells at a given price?

_____

_____

C. Economists use elasticity to predict what consumers will buy. Read the sentences below. Then, using the scale provided, rate the elasticity of the good in each scenario.

1 INELASTIC   2   3   ELASTIC 4

A man buys a blanket at three times the usual cost after an earthquake. _____

A girl buys a skateboard as a gift for her little brother. _____

A college student buys cereal instead of meat and eggs for breakfast. _____

👤 What Do You Think?

D. How does the elasticity of a good at a given price affect whether or not you buy it?

_____

_____

Essential Question Activity

 How do we decide what to buy?

Activity

Complete this activity to answer the Essential Question.

We all make buying decisions on a daily basis. But how strong is our demand for some items? Use the worksheet on the next page to record information about your recent purchases. Include items such as clothing, electronics, food, and entertainment. List the item, its cost, the quantity you purchased, the percentage of your budget that you spent on the item, and whether a substitute was available. You will be asked to share your list.

After you have finished the worksheet, discuss demand as a class. Review the factors that affect demand and create a class list of all the factors that contributed to your decisions.

For example:

· Did you need the item, or did you just want it?

· Was it on sale?

· Did an advertisement influence you?

· Did you buy a substitute item?

Modify

Use the list to analyze your buying decisions. Circle all of the items on the class list that were needs. Eliminate those items from the analysis. Now look at the remaining items. For each item, identify at least one factor that affected your demand. Go back to the Essential Question and write your own answers to these questions:

A. How do I decide what to buy?

B. Could I make better choices?

Item	Quantity	Total cost	Percentage of budget	Substitute available?	Factors influencing your demand

Modify

Respond to questions A and B, given on the previous page.

A. _____

_____

B. _____

_____

Essay

How do we decide what to buy?

Demand describes the actions of buyers, in which they have both the desire to own something and the ability to pay for it. Sellers and economists can often predict consumer demand based on price and changes in other market conditions. Consider the following information:

- According to the U.S. Department of Agriculture, prices on organic goods remain high in many markets as the overall demand for organic products grows.

- According to the World Gold Council, demand for gold was down 16% in the first quarter of 2008. This fall was caused primarily by the sharp rise in the gold price, which briefly touched record levels (above $1,000 per ounce in mid-March).

- According to the City of Tucson Water Department, rainfall plays an important role in daily water demand, particularly during the summer months. Even the hint of rain will cause a significant drop in water demand.

- *The New York Times* published an article in 1918 reporting a strong demand for the immediate construction of thousands of new homes in the Borough of Queens. This was evident by the fact that 75% of the employees of the giant Gas Defense Plant in Queens lived in other boroughs.

- Encouraging sales during December in the United States is proof that demand for toys and games will continue to rise, according to the head of the Trade Development Council's Toys Advisory Committee.

What Do You Think?

What is your opinion? Write a response to the Essential Question, **How do we decide what to buy?** Consider the information above, the Guiding Questions in your textbook, and the activities you have completed in your Journal and at Economics Online, including the WebQuest. See page 183 for a rubric for writing an Essential Question essay.

Don't Forget
Your answer to this question will help you think about the Unit 2 Essential Question: **Who benefits from the free market economy?**

Warmup

 How do suppliers decide what goods and services to offer?

A. Suppose that you are an entrepreneur. You have done some research and found that demand for Product X is greater than the ability of Company X to supply it fully. You decide to start Company Y and produce a competing product, Product Y. How would you decide how much of Product Y to supply? Complete the chart below.

How will you decide the quantity to produce each day?	How will you determine what your production costs will be?
What product or service will I offer? *Product Y—to meet demand and compete with Product X*	
What other factors might affect how much of Product Y you will supply?	How will you decide the price for Product Y?

B. Analyze the following situations as the owner of Company Y. Mark (+) if you think the situation will lead you to increase the supply of Product Y. Mark (–) if you think the situation will lead you to decrease the supply of Product Y.

____ Your production costs decrease.   ____ Your production costs increase.

____ Product X increases in price by 33%.   ____ A new company enters the market, offering a competing product, Product Z.

C. As the owner of Company Y, you see your production costs rising each year. What are some options you would consider for controlling your production costs?

_____

_____

CHAPTER 5 How do suppliers decide what goods and services to offer?

Name: _____

Exploration

I. How Does the Law of Supply Work?

→ Find Out

Supply is the amount of goods available for consumers to buy. The supply schedule below shows how the price of golf balls affects how many golf balls are produced.

Market Supply Schedule

Price Per Golf Ball	Golf Balls Supplied Per Day
$.50	5,000
$1.00	10,000
$1.50	15,000
$2.00	20,000
$2.50	25,000
$3.00	30,000

A. How does the market supply schedule reflect the law of supply?

_____

_____

_____

B. If the price per golf ball was $.25, how might that affect supply, and why?

_____

_____

_____

C. Elasticity of supply shows how companies will respond to changes in the price of a good. List some goods and services in which the supply is elastic or inelastic in the short term. Two examples have been given for you.

Elastic ◁——— *bakery goods*

Inelastic ◁——— *apples*

⬤ What Do You Think?

D. New companies in North America, Europe, and Asia are starting to produce parts for hybrid vehicles. How do you think this trend will affect the supply of hybrids?

_____

_____

CHAPTER 5 How do suppliers decide what goods and
services to offer?

Name: _____

II. Analyzing Production Costs

➔ Find Out

A. For a company to earn profits, its revenue must outweigh its costs. Suppose that
Good Morning is a company that produces hot cereal mixes. Brainstorm Good Morning's
main production costs in the chart below.

Fixed Costs	Variable Costs
• Delivery Trucks	•
•	•
•	•
•	•

B. How would advances in farm technology affect Good Morning's costs, productivity, and
its supply?

_____

_____

_____

C. Good Morning is located in Chicago, Illinois. List at least two more advantages and
two more disadvantages of this location in terms of production costs.

Advantages of Location	Disadvantages
• Good railroad system	• Lots of highway congestion
•	•
•	•

👤 What Do You Think?

D. The hot cereal industry is seasonal (that is, more is sold in the winter). What
could the government do to help companies like Good Morning improve their
year-round business?

_____

_____

CHAPTER 5 How do suppliers decide what goods and services to offer?

Name: _____

III. Exploring Changes in Supply

→ Find Out

A. The supply of oil is inelastic in the short term because oil companies cannot quickly increase output to meet demand. One way consumers react is by finding a substitute. Complete the cause-and-effect chart below. One effect has been filled in for you.

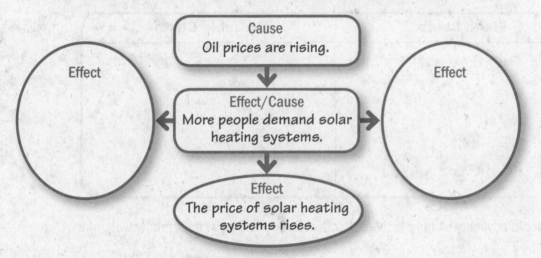

Cause
Oil prices are rising.

Effect

Effect/Cause
More people demand solar heating systems.

Effect

Effect
The price of solar heating systems rises.

B. Suppose that new oil wells are discovered and new oil companies are formed. How would that impact the supply curve in the short term? In the long term?

_____

_____

● What Do You Think?

C. Read the news headlines below. Check those that indicate an impending increase in supply. Put a star next to those that indicate an impending decrease in supply.

New Regulations Issued for Bottled Water

Consumer Prices Soar in June
No End in Sight

Free Trade Pact with Europe Passes

Big Car Closes Its Largest Auto Plant

Subsidies Awarded to Organic Farmers

State Excise Taxes Raised on Trucks

D. Choose one headline above. Write the opening paragraph for the news story that goes with the headline. Your goal is to explain why supply will increase or decrease and how this may affect your readers. Use an additional sheet of paper.

CHAPTER 5 How do suppliers decide what goods and services to offer?

Name: _____

Essential Question Activity

 ## How do suppliers decide what goods and services to offer?

Activity

Complete this activity to answer the Essential Question: How do suppliers decide what goods and services to offer? For this activity, students will act as market researchers and conduct a poll to determine what one good or service their community needs most. Each student will poll three people in the community (family, friends, or other students) to have them identify the one good or service that best serves local needs. When everyone has completed the poll, the class will separate poll results into five different categories: entertainment, food establishments, medical services, recreational facilities, and other. Use the worksheet on the next page to conduct the poll.

Modify

Students will form five marketing groups based on the poll categories. Each group will use the results from the poll in one category to create a description of a business that supplies a good or service that best satisfies the need of the *greater number* of people in the community. Note that two ideas could be combined to create one business. Check against listings in the telephone directory or Chamber of Commerce to determine if a similar business already exists in the community. Since a supplier needs an incentive, students should consider the necessity of the business turning a profit. Student groups will then present their business ideas to the class and ask students to vote for the one business plan from the five categories that is most likely to be successful. After students have made their selections, have them answer the following questions:

A. Why do you think the business you chose would have a greater chance of success?

B. Would you invest in this business? Why?

C. Can you identify some fixed or variable costs for this business?

D. How might the government regulate this good or service?

As a final exercise, present the choices from the original poll to a different class. Ask those students to vote on the product or service they think would benefit the majority of people in the community. Then ask the students from this class to answer questions A and B.

CHAPTER 5 How do suppliers decide what goods and services to offer?

Name: _____

Ask three people in the community the poll questions below and record their answers in the spaces provided.

Community Needs Poll

Instructions: Before you ask the poll questions, tell each person you are interviewing that you are taking an anonymous poll (that is, no names will be used). Let them know that this poll is for a school activity. **Questions to Ask:**	Person 1	Person 2	Person 3
1. What is your age?			
2. Are you male or female?			
3. What is your occupation? (Write *student*, if a student.)			
4. What is the one good, or product, that your community needs most?			
5. What is the one service that your community needs most?			
6. Which one—the good or the service—does your community need most?			
7. Explain your choice for question 6. Why did you choose this one?			

Modify

Use another sheet of paper to complete the Modify section given on the previous page.

CHAPTER 5 How do suppliers decide what goods and services to offer?

Name: _____

Essay

 ## How do suppliers decide what goods and services to offer?

The law of supply may seem simple—producers offer more of something as its price increases and less as its price decreases. Deciding exactly how much to produce, however, is a complex process in real life. So, how do suppliers meet demand? Consider these situations:

- With a one-year surge in supply and a number of new farms starting up, organic milk is suddenly an affordable alternative to conventional milk. One leading organic milk company, however, forecast downward earnings due to "a significant near-term industry-wide oversupply of raw organic milk."

- A foreign country's Ministry of Agriculture and Forestry (MAF) released future wood availability figures that predict a steady increase in supply over the next 12 years. "There are growing markets for wood and wood energy products," said a senior analyst with MAF. "There is also opportunity for investment in expanding the capacity of existing mills and in building new mills."

- The U.S. Centers for Disease Control and Prevention (CDC) hopes to avoid last year's supply-line nightmare in which elderly and other high-risk people waited in lines for hours to receive flu shots. The shortage of flu shots occurred when one producer failed to make its promised number of doses. A rise in the number of vaccine manufacturers offers hope that this year's supply will meet demand.

Should suppliers provide goods and services based only on the market? What happens when necessary or desired goods and services are not readily available to consumers?

What Do You Think?

What is your opinion? Write a response to the Essential Question, **How do suppliers decide what goods and services to offer?** Consider your thoughts on the situations above, the Guiding Questions in your textbook, and the activities you have completed in your Journal and at Economics Online, including the WebQuest. See page 183 for a rubric for writing an Essential Question essay.

 Don't Forget

Your answer to this question will help you think about the Unit 2 Essential Question: **Who benefits from the free market economy?**

Name: _____

Warmup

 ## What is the right price?

A. As a consumer, how do you decide whether the price of a good is right? What are the three most important actions you might take to help you decide? Number them in order.

____ Compare prices on the Internet. ____ Read a product review.

____ Compare prices in catalogs. ____ Survey your friends.

____ Visit two to four stores. ____ Visit five to ten stores.

B. What other factors might help you decide?

_____

_____

_____

_____

C. How does a seller determine the right price? What do you think are the three most important factors? Number them in order.

____ Cost of raw materials ____ Cost of labor

____ Available substitutes ____ Competition

____ Taxes ____ Market research

D. A baseball bat signed by a famous player is sold for $1500. A similar bat without any signature sold for $70. Speculate on why this is.

_____

_____

_____

_____

_____

Exploration

I. Price Equilibrium and Disequilibrium

→ Find Out

A. Price is not static. It goes up or down under different conditions. Complete the chart by explaining what you know about price, supply, and demand in each situation. The first row has been completed for you.

Price	Supply	Demand
Equilibrium	Equal	Equal
	High supply; surplus	
Low price		
Price floor		
		High demand

B. Why might an economist think that price floors hurt the economy?

_____

_____

👤 What Do You Think?

C. The National Organ Transplant Act of 1984 prohibits the sale of human organs. Why do you think the government forbids the sale of human organs?

_____

_____

_____

Name: _____

II. Balance in the Marketplace

→ Find Out

A. Table 1 below shows the combined supply and demand schedule for a new model of sunglasses. Plot the supply and demand curves on the grid below. Circle the equilibrium price.

Table 1

Price	Quantity Demanded	Quantity Supplied
$50	50	250
$40	100	200
$30	150	150
$20	200	100
$10	250	50

Table 2

Price	Quantity Demanded
$50	150
$40	200
$30	250
$20	300
$10	350

Title: _____

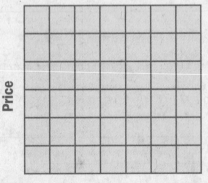

Price

Label: _____

B. You bought those sunglasses for $35. Did you get a bargain? How do you know?

_____

_____

_____

C. The sunglasses become a fad. The new demand schedule points can be found in Table 2. Plot the new demand curve. Circle the new equilibrium price.

👤 What Do You Think?

D. A friend is desperate for a pair of those popular sunglasses. What advice would you give your friend about buying them?

_____

_____

_____

III. Changes in the Marketplace

→ Find Out

A. The price of bottled water varies in the summer. Think about each scenario below, then fill out the causes and effects. The first one has been completed for you.

July: Too much bottled water hits the market during a cool spell.

Cause — Demand for bottled water is low. → SURPLUS → Effect — Stores have extra bottles; price falls.

August: Groundwater is contaminated during a hurricane. The government steps in to control bottled water supplies.

Cause → RATIONING → Effect

September: The government does not have enough bottled water for everyone.

Cause → BLACK MARKET → Effect

👤 What Do You Think?

B. Under what circumstances would a supplier of bottled water increase its output? Why?

_____

_____

_____

C. How is price a language for buyers and sellers?

_____

_____

_____

Name: _____

IV. Informed Choices: Price and Quality

👤 What Do You Think?

For a consumer, cost can be one of several factors in deciding on a purchase. How do you decide what to buy?

Granola Bar Guide					
			☹️ 😐 🙂 😁		
			poor - great		
Brand	**Price/Box**	**Crunch**	**Fruit/Nuts**	**Taste**	**Nutrition**
Chock O' Cherries	$4.75	😐	😁	😐	😐
Tasty Treat	$6.75	🙂	😐	😁	☹️
Nut 'N Crunch	$6.00	🙂	🙂	🙂	🙂

A. You want to buy a box of granola bars to bring on a trip. Study the above chart. How do you decide which type of granola bar is right for you?

_____

_____

B. What factors do you consider when you buy goods? Rate the factors from one (most important) to four (least important).

Technology: _____ price _____ quality _____ style _____ ease of use

Clothes: _____ fit _____ price _____ style _____ practicality

Food: _____ taste _____ nutrition _____ price _____ convenience

C. How do your choices as a consumer affect the market for granola bars, technology, clothes, or other goods?

_____

_____

_____

Essential Question Activity

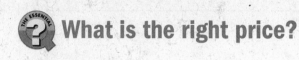 **What is the right price?**

Activity

Complete this activity to answer the Essential Question.

Suppose that your class is planning to sell T-shirts to raise funds for disaster relief in a nearby community. Using the worksheet on the next page, gather the following information:

A. What is the cost of buying 1,000 plain, white T-shirts in bulk?

B. What is the cost of having a special design printed on the shirts?

C. What is the average price that stores in your area charge for a printed T-shirt?

Using this information, decide what price you think people would be willing to pay for a T-shirt. You need to make enough money above your costs to make a donation. When you have made your decision, fill in your price on the worksheet. Write an explanation of how you arrived at the right price.

Modify

You have set your price and begun selling your T-shirts. Now, choose two of the following situations. Describe how each of them might cause you to modify your plan:

A. Another school begins selling similar T-shirts for a dollar less than your price.

B. After a week, you have not sold enough T-shirts to cover what you spent to buy and print the shirts.

C. A local news broadcast raises questions about whether disaster relief funds are being spent wisely.

Name: _____

Item	Source	Cost
A. 1,000 plain white T-shirts	1. 2. 3.	1. 2. 3.
B. Special "printed-on" design	1. 2. 3.	1. 2. 3.
C. T-shirt prices	1. 2. 3.	1. 2. 3. Average T-shirt price:

At what price will you sell each T-shirt? _____

How much can you give to the disaster relief fund from the sale of each T-shirt? _____

How much will you be able to donate if you sell every T-shirt? _____

How did you decide on the selling price?

_____

_____

_____

Modify

Respond to two of the situations given on the previous page.

_____

_____

_____

_____

Essay

What is the right price?

At its core, a price is the point at which someone is willing to sell something, and someone else is willing to buy it. Price is a signal to both buyers and sellers in the marketplace; it affects the distribution of resources. How might one's values or perspective affect one's view about the role of price in the marketplace? Consider these situations:

- High-priced vacation home Web sites drive up the cost of land, making housing unaffordable for year-round residents.

- A surgeon charges $150,000 for one operation.

- A bathing suit goes on sale at 25% off after July 4th and 50% off on August 1.

- Picasso's *Garçon à la pipe* sells at auction for $104,000,000.

- In the course of one year, milk prices rise 25%.

- Speculators drive up the price of wheat, affecting the worldwide cost of bread.

- A community restricts ocean access to those who can afford to join a beach club.

When is a price right? Should it always depend solely on the equilibrium point of supply and demand? Or are some things priceless and should always be free?

What Do You Think?

What is your opinion? Write a response to the Essential Question, **What is the right price?** Consider your thoughts on the situations above, the Guiding Questions in your textbook, and the activities you have completed in your Journal and at Economics Online, including the WebQuest. See page 183 for a rubric for writing an Essential Question essay.

Don't Forget

Your answer to this question will help you think about the Unit 2 Essential Question: **Who benefits from the free market economy?**

CHAPTER 7 Market Structures

Warmup

 How does competition affect your choices?

A. Sellers want consumers to buy their products instead of those of their competitors. What do you think are the five most influential factors when it comes to consumer choice? Number your top five choices from **1** (most important) to **5** (fifth most important).

___ Location of stores	___ Advertising	___ Price
___ Product features	___ Style options	___ Safety
___ Customer service	___ Flexible payment options	___ Durability
___ Designer brand name	___ Latest technology	___ Atmosphere
___ Reward programs	___ Quality	___ Value
___ Available alternatives	___ Environmentally friendly	___ Ease of use

B. How would your priorities change, depending on the product you're buying? Write the two most influential factors from the list above for:

Buying a new car   _____   _____

Choosing a restaurant   _____   _____

Buying a new computer   _____   _____

Getting an oil change   _____   _____

C. After years of research, Company V revolutionizes the vacuum cleaner industry using nanotechnology. The firm refuses to share its discovery with its competitors. Soon, Company V's new vacuum cleaners fly off the store shelves. Other vacuum cleaner companies claim that Company V is using unfair business practices by not sharing its discovery. Do you agree? Why or why not?

_____

_____

_____

_____

_____

Name: _____

Exploration

I. Analyzing Perfect Competition

➡ Find Out

A. Are the suppliers below part of a perfectly competitive market? Evaluate each business by drawing an *X* in the appropriate boxes to show that the firm meets that condition of perfect competition. One example has been done for you.

Business	Many Buyers and Sellers	Identical Product	Informed Buyers/Sellers	Free Market Entry/Exit
Lemonade stands	X	X	X	X
Car dealers				
Pumpkin farmers				
Movie theaters				

B. What barriers might prevent new commercial airline companies from entering the market?

_____

_____

C. In a perfectly competitive market, consumers have a lot of choices and low prices. Circle the products below that are commodities bought and sold in perfect competition. Then, brainstorm to add five more commodities.

gold	wheat	furniture	rice	computers
DVDs	perfume	apples	concert tickets	heating oil

_____   _____   _____   _____

👤 What Do You Think?

D. Who benefits more from perfect competition—buyers or sellers? Why?

_____

_____

Name: _____

II. Monopolies

→ Find Out

A. Complete the chart below with details about monopolies. Some information has been filled in for you.

> In a *monopoly*, a single seller controls the entire market for a good or service.

Reasons monopolies form:	Economic characteristics:	Examples of monopolies:
• The good or service has no close substitute.	• A monopolist's marginal revenue is lower than the market price.	• Natural monopoly
•	•	•
•	•	•

👤 What Do You Think?

B. Do you agree or disagree with the statements below? Circle the number that best reflects your opinion.

1 = Strongly Disagree; 2 = Disagree; 3 = Neutral; 4 = Agree; 5 = Strongly Agree

■ Price discrimination is unfair to consumers.	1 2 3 4 5
■ Patents should not have an expiration date.	1 2 3 4 5
■ Natural monopolies should be regulated by the government.	1 2 3 4 5
■ The government should break up all monopolies.	1 2 3 4 5
■ Consumers should not buy goods or services from a monopolist.	1 2 3 4 5
■ Monopolies reduce consumer choices.	1 2 3 4 5

C. Choose one statement from Part B. Give reasons for your opinion.

_____

_____

_____

_____

III. The Role of Monopolistic Competition and Oligopoly

➔ Find Out

A. Think about how different market structures affect competition. Read each characteristic below. Then, number the market structures, from lowest to highest, based on how they affect that characteristic. The first one has been done for you. The market structure that sets the lowest prices is marked **L**. The market structure that sets the highest prices is marked **H**. Oligopoly falls somewhere in between, so it's marked **IB**.

Prices

_H_ Monopoly 　　　　　　 _L_ Monopolistic Competition 　　　　 _IB_ Oligopoly

Output

___ Perfect Competition 　　　 ___ Monopoly 　　　　　　 ___ Monopolistic Competition

Profits

___ Perfect Competition 　　　 ___ Monopoly 　　　　　　 ___ Oligopoly

Barriers to Entry

___ Perfect Competition 　　 ___ Monopolistic Competition 　　 ___ Oligopoly

Number of Firms

___ Monopoly 　　　　　　 ___ Monopolistic Competition 　　　 ___ Oligopoly

B. In what ways do consumers benefit from nonprice competition?

_____

_____

_____

👤 What Do You Think?

C. If an oligopoly exists in a specific industry, should the government take steps to make the industry more competitive? Why or why not?

_____

_____

D. What might happen to consumers if the U.S. government did not regulate oligopolies, such as car makers?

_____

_____

Name: _____

IV. Regulation and Deregulation

Find Out

A. How do firms try to control the price and total output of goods in a given market? What does the U.S. government do to promote competition? Complete the chart below.

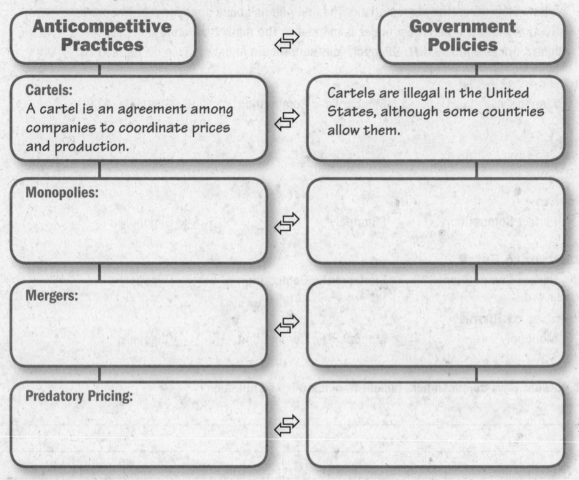

Anticompetitive Practices ⇄ **Government Policies**

Anticompetitive Practices	Government Policies
Cartels: A cartel is an agreement among companies to coordinate prices and production.	Cartels are illegal in the United States, although some countries allow them.
Monopolies:	
Mergers:	
Predatory Pricing:	

What Do You Think?

B. Under what circumstances should the government regulate industries that are not natural monopolies?

_____

_____

C. Review the information about airlines in your textbook. In your opinion, what is the future of the airline industry? Should the business practices of major airlines be even more regulated? Explain.

_____

_____

Essential Question Activity

 How does competition affect your choices?

Activity

Complete this activity to answer the Essential Question.

To welcome a new student and inform them about the goods and services available in the community, the class will create a newcomer's kit. To create this kit, the class will generate a list of businesses that provide goods and services that would be helpful to a new student. The list will identify categories of goods and services such as fast food, clothing, sporting goods, entertainment, and automobile services. Use the worksheet on the next page to gather information about the products or services. Then use the worksheet to answer the following questions:

A. Which categories have the greatest number of choices? Is there a wide range of prices?

B. Give one example of nonprice differentiation between products in a category.

C. Identify the market structure for each business.

Modify

The class will use the information they have gathered to create a mini-business directory. Each business on the list will have an entry that provides basic information such as the name of the business, and its street or Web address. Entries for each business will highlight the type of goods or services that the business provides and their price range. Each entry should also include a rating. The rating could be in the form of a one to two sentence review. Or, students can create a rating system with a key that explains what the rating symbols mean. Students will also create a map for the directory that shows the locations of all the businesses. When the directory is finished, give it to the school guidance office so that it can be distributed to students who are new to the area.

Name: _____

Newcomer's Kit Worksheet

	Address, Phone, URL	Products/Services	Prices	Nonprice Differentiantion
Auto Services 1. _____ 2. _____	1. _____ 2. _____	1. _____ 2. _____	1. _____ 2. _____	1. _____ 2. _____
Clothing 1. _____ 2. _____	1. _____ 2. _____	1. _____ 2. _____	1. _____ 2. _____	1. _____ 2. _____
Entertainment 1. _____ 2. _____	1. _____ 2. _____	1. _____ 2. _____	1. _____ 2. _____	1. _____ 2. _____
Food & Snacks 1. _____ 2. _____	1. _____ 2. _____	1. _____ 2. _____	1. _____ 2. _____	1. _____ 2. _____
Sporting Goods 1. _____ 2. _____	1. _____ 2. _____	1. _____ 2. _____	1. _____ 2. _____	1. _____ 2. _____
Other 1. _____ 2. _____	1. _____ 2. _____	1. _____ 2. _____	1. _____ 2. _____	1. _____ 2. _____

Use a code to indicate market structure (for example: **** = perfect competition; *** = monopolistic competition; ** = oligopoly; * = monopoly).

Make additional copies of this worksheet as needed. Use another sheet of paper for the Modify section.

Essay

How does competition affect your choices?

As a consumer, you make choices every day. In some situations, however, you have considerably more choices than in others. Consider these situations:

- You go for a snack in the vending machine, only to find that every slot is filled with products from one snack-food company.

- Two pharmacy stores are located across the street from one another. One advertises on a giant banner that it honors the other store's coupons.

- Your printer is out of ink. Replacement ink can only be purchased through the printer company's Web site.

- You want to buy an airline ticket to visit relatives in a distant state. One airline offers the lowest fare, but another airline has more convenient flight times. A third airline offers a meal and more leg room.

- On a restaurant menu, you see that the price of an entrée is $15. However, for senior citizens, the same entrée costs just $10. Kids 10 and under eat for free.

- A national bookstore chain just opened a branch in a nearby shopping plaza. Six months later, the last independent bookstore downtown goes out of business.

- It's time to do your weekly grocery shopping. You see signs for a local farmers market on the way to the grocery store.

- You move into a new neighborhood where only one company offers Internet service.

What Do You Think?

What is your opinion? Write a response to the Essential Question, **How does competition affect your choices?** Consider the situations above, the Guiding Questions in your textbook, and the activities you have completed in your Journal and at Economics Online, including the WebQuest. See page 183 for a rubric for writing an Essential Question essay.

Don't Forget

Your answer to this question will help you think about the Unit 2 Essential Question: **Who benefits from the free market economy?**

UNIT 2 — How Markets Work

Essay Warmup

Examine the following perspectives on markets. The questions that follow each perspective will help you focus your thinking on the Unit 2 Essential Question, **Who benefits from the free market economy?**

> I suspect ignorance about economics leads many to believe that when two people exchange goods and money, one wins and the other loses. If rich capitalists profit, the poor and the weak suffer. That's a myth. How many times have you paid $1 for a cup of coffee and after the clerk said, "thank you," you responded, "thank you"? There's a wealth of economics wisdom in the weird double thank-you moment. Why does it happen? Because you want the coffee more than the buck, and the store wants the buck more than the coffee. Both of you win.
>
> —*John Stossel,* Real Clear Politics.com, *"The Double Thank-You Moment",* May 30, 2007

A. According to the author, what can be the result of ignorance about economics?

_____

_____

B. How can making a purchase benefit the buyer and the seller?

_____

_____

> I'm all for a free economy, but competitors need to play by some rules. Congress has the power to regulate this trade through the commerce clause of the Constitution and needs to begin to do so.
>
> —*Gatsby 999* msnbc.com

C. What kind of economy does this author think the United States should have? Explain.

_____

_____

_____

_____

D. What does this cartoon say about who benefits from a free market society?

_____

_____

_____

E. Do you agree with the cartoonist's point of view?

_____

_____

_____

👤 What Do You Think?

Choose one of the documents above and explain how it helps you answer the
Unit 2 Essential Question, **Who benefits from the free market economy?**

_____

_____

_____

_____

_____

_____

_____

UNIT 2 How Markets Work

Essay

 Who benefits from the free market economy?

Write an essay in response to the Unit 2 Essential Question. Use your answers to the Essential Question warmup on the previous pages, your answers to the chapter Essential Questions, and what you have learned in the unit. Keep in mind that your essay should reflect your thoughtful and well-supported personal point of view. Filling in the chart below will help you structure your essay. Go to page 183 for a rubric for writing an Essential Question essay.

Thesis Statement: _____

_____

Body Paragraph 1	Body Paragraph 2	Body Paragraph 3
Main Idea _____ _____ _____ _____	**Main Idea** _____ _____ _____ _____	**Main Idea** _____ _____ _____ _____
Supporting Details 1. _____ _____ _____ 2. _____ _____ _____ 3. _____ _____ _____	**Supporting Details** 1. _____ _____ _____ 2. _____ _____ _____ 3. _____ _____ _____	**Supporting Details** 1. _____ _____ _____ 2. _____ _____ _____ 3. _____ _____ _____

Conclusion: _____

_____

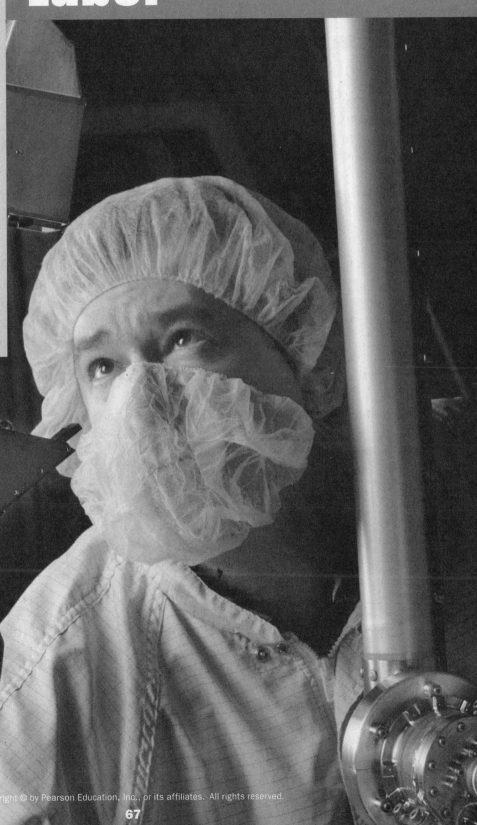

Unit **3**

Business and Labor

Chapter 8
Essential Question

Why do some businesses succeed and others fail?

Chapter 9
Essential Question

How can workers best meet the challenges of a changing economy?

Name: _____

UNIT 3 Business and Labor

Warmup

How can businesses and labor best achieve their goals?

Think about your local economy—the businesses in your city or town, the types of jobs people have, and so on. All across the country, businesses and workers such as these form the foundation of our national economy. In Unit 3, you will study business organizations and labor and explore responses to the Unit Essential Question.

Volunteers are essential to the success of many nonprofit organizations.

Read this business scenario and answer the following questions.
Kaya had long dreamed of opening a natural foods store. She had a passion for healthy eating and was trained as a nutritionist. After a long period of researching possible locations, local competition, and ways to organize her business, Kaya felt ready to open her store. She created a business plan, setting out her financial goals for the next five years. In the first year, her store, called Naturally Delicious, exceeded its profit goals by eight percent.

A. List three reasons why Naturally Delicious was a success.

1. _____

2. _____

3. _____

B. Suppose that you wanted to apply for a part-time job as a clerk at Naturally Delicious. What skills and experiences would you need?

_____

_____

C. Suppose that you were an investor. Kaya has decided to open another Naturally Delicious store in a nearby city. Would you invest in this store? Why or why not?

_____

_____

Warmup

 Why do some businesses succeed and others fail?

A. What qualities are most important for someone who wants to start his or her own business? Place a check mark next to the three qualities you think are most important.

___ good leader	___ hard worker	___ support from family/friends
___ team player	___ risk taker	___ business school graduate
___ optimistic	___ high energy level	___ business experience
___ innovative	___ good with numbers	___ good with details

B. Choose one of the qualities you checked above. Explain why you think this quality is important in a person who wants to begin a new business.

_____

_____

_____

_____

C. Sole proprietorships make up more than 70 percent of business organizations in the United States. Yet, they only account for about 4 percent of sales. On the other hand, corporations make up about 20 percent of businesses, but more than 80 percent of sales. Why do you think this is so?

_____

_____

_____

_____

Exploration

I. The Business of Sole Proprietorships

➡ Find Out

When an entrepreneur has an idea for a new business, he or she usually writes a business plan. (In brief, business plans are used to organize ideas, to see whether a new business will be a success, and to present to lenders or investors when looking for capital.) Read the summary, at right, of a business plan for a sole proprietorship, and then answer the questions that follow.

> Sal decides to open a movie theater in a small-sized city that will show independent films and serve expanded food options, including dinner. There are two large theaters within 30 miles of this city, but they both show only the most popular movies and neither serves dinner. Sal has $50,000 saved and hopes to raise additional capital by taking out a $50,000 small business loan. Sal's close friend plans to work at the theater 30 hours a week.

A. What are the minimum requirements that Sal must meet to start this sole proprietorship?

_____

_____

👤 What Do You Think?

B. What do you think are some advantages that Sal has in forming a sole proprietorship for this business?

_____

_____

C. What do you think are some disadvantages that Sal has to overcome for this sole proprietorship to be successful?

_____

_____

D. Do you think Sal's movie theater is more likely to succeed or to fail? Explain.

_____

_____

_____

II. Types of Partnerships

→ Find Out

A. What are the risks and benefits of forming different kinds of partnerships? Complete the concept webs below.

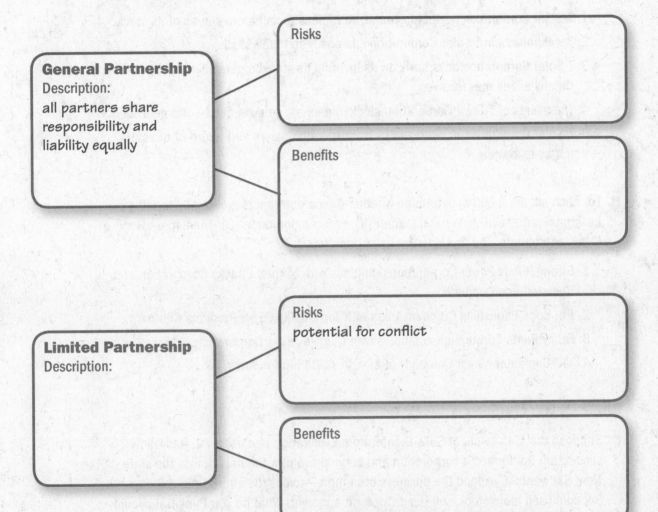

General Partnership
Description:
all partners share
responsibility and
liability equally

Risks

Benefits

Limited Partnership
Description:

Risks
potential for conflict

Benefits

👤 What Do You Think?

B. What is a limited liability partnership? Why do you think only people who work in occupations such as lawyers and doctors are allowed to form this type of partnership?

_____

_____

_____

_____

III. Exploring the Corporate World

→ Find Out

A. For each situation below, mark **+** if being a corporation is an advantage in this case or mark **−** if being a corporation is a disadvantage. The first one has been done for you.

_+_ 1. T-Solar Corporation wants to expand, so it plans to sell more shares of its stock.

___ 2. Stockholders in T-Solar Corporation can easily sell their stock.

___ 3. T-Solar Corporation pays taxes on its income. Its stockholders also pay taxes on the dividends they receive.

___ 4. The assets of T-Solar Corporation stockholders are safe even if T-Solar gets sued.

___ 5. T-Solar Corporation is managed by its corporate officers and board of directors, not by its owners.

B. For each situation below, determine whether the corporation is growing by forming a horizontal merger (H), a vertical merger (V), or a conglomerate (C). Then, mark **H, V,** or **C,** as appropriate. The first one has been done for you.

_C_ 1. Strong Winds Power Corporation combines with Natural Snacks Corporation and Recycled Pen Company.

___ 2. Big Book Publishing Company joins with Top Quality Paper Products Company.

___ 3. Fancy Pants Corporation combines with Rugged Jeans Corporation.

___ 4. XYZ Computer Maker Company joins with ABC Chip Producer, Inc.

☺ What Do You Think?

C. Suppose that Sal, owner of Sal's Theater from Exploration I on page 70, was wildly successful. Sal formed a corporation and opened five new theaters across the state. Now, Sal wants to expand the business even more—across the entire United States. Sal could sell more stock, sell bonds, or form a merger. What do you think Sal should do, and why?

_____

_____

_____

_____

_____

CHAPTER 8 Why do some businesses succeed and others fail?

Name: _____

IV. Choosing the Right Business Organization

➔ Find Out

A. Entrepreneurs have to make decisions about which kind of business organization they want to use when starting a business. What factors are most important when deciding which business organization to use? Rank the following choices from 1 (most important) to 6 (least important).

____ resources available to start business   ____ desire to share profits and decision-making

____ amount of past experience in business   ____ length of time desired to be in business

____ willingness to be subject to regulations   ____ level of personal liability desired

B. Explain why you chose your #1 factor above.

_____

_____

👤 What Do You Think?

C. Suppose that you are working as a business consultant, helping entrepreneurs who want to start their own businesses. For each of the scenarios below, provide advice about which form of business organization you would recommend and your reasons why.

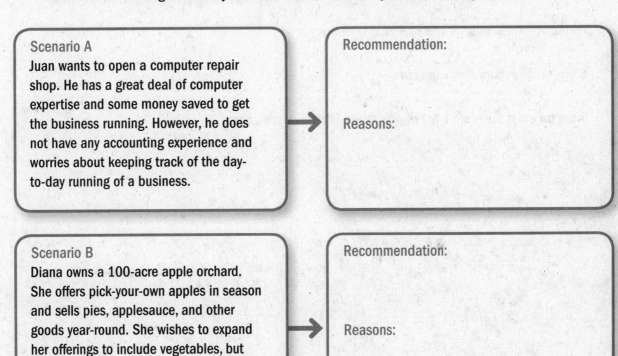

Scenario A
Juan wants to open a computer repair shop. He has a great deal of computer expertise and some money saved to get the business running. However, he does not have any accounting experience and worries about keeping track of the day-to-day running of a business.

Recommendation:

Reasons:

Scenario B
Diana owns a 100-acre apple orchard. She offers pick-your-own apples in season and sells pies, applesauce, and other goods year-round. She wishes to expand her offerings to include vegetables, but does not have the acreage or knowledge to grow them herself.

Recommendation:

Reasons:

Essential Question Activity

 Why do some businesses succeed and others fail?

Activity

Complete one of the following activities to answer the Essential Question.

A. Conduct an interview with either a current or former sole proprietor, partner in a partnership, manager of a corporation, or a franchisee to uncover their personal view of the pros and cons of doing business. Focus on why he or she thought the business succeeded or failed.

B. Using information on the Internet or in a business magazine or newspaper, such as *The Wall Street Journal,* research why a specific entrepreneur or business succeeded or failed.

Use the worksheet on the next page to guide your information gathering.

Modify

In groups of three or four students, share the specific information that you gathered. Then, as a group:

· Formulate a response to the Essential Question.

· Share your response with the class.

· Work together to create a list of guidelines for business success.

Information Gathering Worksheet

Interview with: _____

Date of interview(s): _____

or

Online/print source (include URL, if applicable): _____
_____

Date(s) of publication/online searches: _____

Name of business and/or business owner: _____

Type of business organization: _____

Number of years in business/date founded: _____

Description of business: _____
_____

Check the most accurate description of the business to date:

__ Business has been successful, making steady profits.

__ Business has lost money, but is still running.

__ Business failed and is no longer running.

__ Other: _____

Reasons why business succeeded or failed: _____
_____
_____
_____
_____

Other important information: _____
_____
_____
_____

Modify

List your guidelines for business success:

_____
_____
_____
_____

Essay

Why do some businesses succeed and others fail?

Entrepreneurs can choose any number of ways to organize their businesses, each of which has its own advantages and disadvantages. Choosing the right organization for a certain business idea is one way to ensure success; other factors come into play as well. Do good planning and organization always determine success, or do luck and unforeseen circumstances also play a part? Consider these situations:

- Tanya opens a small bookshop on a busy main street. Six months later, a large chain bookstore opens three blocks away.

- Two people form a partnership to start a landscaping business. The business runs well until one of the partners falls ill.

- Tony researches different kinds of cheeses and their marketability for over a year before opening his cheese shop. In the first year, he exceeds his projected profits by 10 percent.

- A sole proprietor struggles to keep the business afloat because of an inability to keep the accounting up to date.

- Three physicians operate a clinic together, which they have registered as a limited liability partnership. One of the doctors is sued for malpractice.

- A toy company is accused of using toxic paint on its toys, and its stock prices plummet.

What Do You Think?

What is your opinion? Write a response to the Essential Question, **Why do some businesses succeed and others fail?** Consider the situations above, the Guiding Questions in your textbook, and the activities you have completed in your Journal and at Economics Online, including the WebQuest. See page 183 for a rubric for writing an Essential Question essay.

> **Don't Forget**
> Your answer to this question will help you think about the Unit 3 Essential Question: **How can businesses and labor best achieve their goals?**

CHAPTER **9** **Labor**

Warmup

How can workers best meet the challenges of a changing economy?

A. Think about the ways jobs have changed throughout history. Then, complete the outer circles of the concept web with information about the various jobs three adults you know have had in the past. For example, you may want to interview aunts, uncles, and grandparents about the different jobs they had in the 1960s, 1970s, and so on.

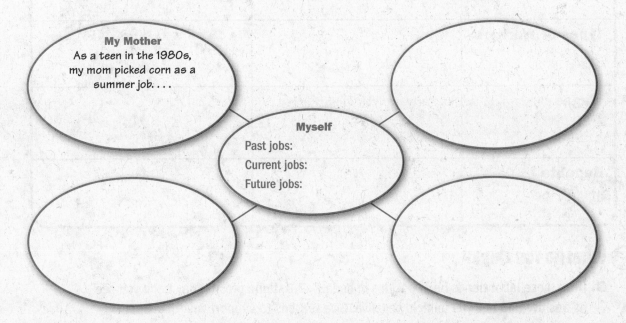

My Mother
As a teen in the 1980s, my mom picked corn as a summer job. . . .

Myself
Past jobs:
Current jobs:
Future jobs:

B. Finish creating your concept web by filling in the "Myself" circle. Include jobs you have held in the past and hold currently, as well as jobs you would like to have in the future.

C. What do you notice about the jobs people had in the past? Does your concept web reflect any industry changes or historical trends?

_____

_____

D. What challenges might you face in the future jobs you listed? How might you deal with those challenges?

_____

_____

CHAPTER 9 How can workers best meet the challenges
of a changing economy?

Name: _____

Exploration

I. Looking at Labor Trends

⊳ Find Out

A. New technology, wars, and other factors have all affected the United States labor force over the past 100 years. Fill in the chart with examples of how trends have changed in each category. Some examples are given.

	Trends in the Past	**Trends Today**
Types of Jobs		more service and technology jobs
Types of Workers		
Wages	steady growth in earnings	
Benefits		

⊖ What Do You Think?

B. Have these labor trends been positive or negative? List one present-day trend you see as positive and one you think is negative. Give reasons to support your opinions.

Positive trend: _____

_____

_____

Negative trend: _____

_____

_____

C. Would you rather have been a worker in the labor force 100 years ago or a worker in today's labor market? Explain.

_____

_____

CHAPTER 9 How can workers best meet the
challenges of a changing economy?

Name: _____

II. How Wages Are Determined

What Do You Think?

Education is a major factor in determining how much money a person earns. However, other factors, such as race and gender, may affect wage levels, too. Study the following wage statistics for selected occupations.

Occupation	Required Education Level	Median Annual Earnings, 2007
Dentist	college graduate, plus dental school	$137,630
Technical writer	college graduate	$60,390
Accountant	college graduate	$57,060
Surgical technologist	1–3 years beyond high school*	$37,540
Payroll clerk	high school graduate	$33,810
Roofer	less than 4 years high school	$33,240
Cook	less than 4 years high school	$21,220

Source: U.S. Bureau of Labor Statistics

*Includes graduates of community and technical colleges

A. The learning effect says that more education results in higher wages. The screening effect says a college degree identifies people who are likely to be good workers. Explain how this chart supports both the learning effect and the screening effect.

_____

_____

B. About 50 percent of workers in an occupation earn less than the median wage for that job, and about 50 percent earn more. For the following examples, write an "L" if wages would likely be lower than the median annual earnings as shown in the chart above. Write an "H" if wages would likely be higher.

___ female surgical technologist   ___ accountant with 30 years experience

___ payroll clerk with college degree   ___ dentist in a low demand market

C. How does labor supply and demand affect wages? Explain how the equilibrium wage would be affected in the following situations.

A local restaurant is hiring a new cook, and you are one of many applicants for the job.

_____

_____

You are one of only a few roofers in a town when a storm damages many properties.

_____

_____

CHAPTER 9 How can workers best meet the challenges
of a changing economy?

Name: _____

III. Challenges for Workers

⇨ Find Out

A. Complete the chart below with an explanation of how each topic presents a
challenge to workers in the United States.

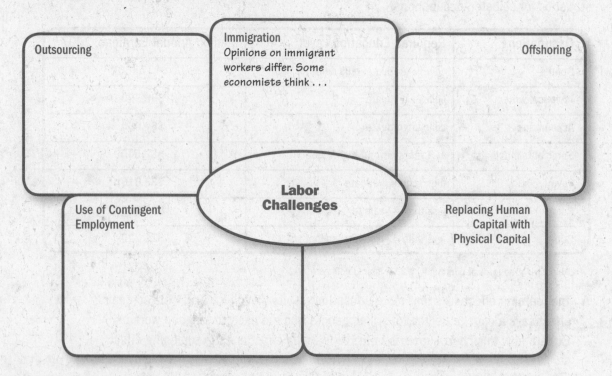

Outsourcing

Immigration
Opinions on immigrant
workers differ. Some
economists think . . .

Offshoring

Use of Contingent
Employment

**Labor
Challenges**

Replacing Human
Capital with
Physical Capital

B. One way workers address challenges, such as those above, is by forming or joining labor
unions. People have different views on the benefits of unions, however. List at least two
advantages and two disadvantages of labor unions.

Labor Union Pros	Labor Union Cons

🙍 What Do You Think?

C. What challenge do you think affects workers the most today? Will this challenge also affect
them in the future? Explain.

_____

_____

CHAPTER 9 How can workers best meet the challenges of a changing economy?

Name: _____

Essential Question Activity

How can workers best meet the challenges of a changing economy?

Activity

Complete this activity to answer the Essential Question.

People who have successful careers know that their success depends on being able to plan ahead. Preparation helps to overcome setbacks, such as a job layoff, or if new technology makes skills obsolete. It also helps to be ready in case you start a family and need to have a job that helps meet your financial needs.

Think about the kind of careers that interest you the most. Identify your interests and potential careers using the worksheet on the next page.

Modify

Review your completed career worksheet. Then research trends in the U.S. and global economy that will have an impact on your future career.

The trends listed below are seen by many economists as posing some of the greatest challenges for workers in the future.

· Climate Change

· Global Trade

· Speed of Technological Change

· Rise of Megacities

· Shifts in World Populations

· Genetic Engineering

Explain how your career choices will prepare you to meet those challenges.

CHAPTER 9 How can workers best meet the challenges
of a changing economy?

Name: _____

What are your goals in life? List your goals for education, family, income, retirement, and so
on below. Then, think about how you can reach these goals as an adult.

Educational Goals:	Family Goals:	Income Goals:	Retirement Goals:	Educational Goals:	Other Goals:

Now, think about the kinds of careers or businesses that interest you the most.
Then, complete the chart below.

	1.	2.	3.	4.
What four career/ business fields interest me most?				
Why am I interested in each career/ business?				
What do I need to do to prepare for each career/business?				
What is the future outlook for each career/business?				
What else do I know, or need to know, about each career/ business?				
What is the median annual wage for jobs in these fields?				

Which of your potential careers do you think would be the best choice for you? Why?

_____

_____

Use the U.S. Bureau of Labor Statistics website (www.bls.gov) to find out the median
annual wage for each of your potential careers. Add this information to your chart.
Does this change which career you chose as your top choice? Why or why not?

_____

_____

Modify

Explain how your career choices will prepare you to meet any or all of the challenges listed
on the previous page. Use another sheet of paper.

CHAPTER 9 How can workers best meet the challenges of a changing economy?

Name: _____

Essay

How can workers best meet the challenges of a changing economy?

Like businesses, workers must also adapt to the many economic challenges ahead of them. The choices each worker makes today will affect their lives tomorrow—and in the future. Consider the following information from the U.S. Bureau of Labor Statistics:

■ A little more than 50 percent of American workers receive health care benefits. About 20 percent of American workers take part in defined-benefit pension plans (these are retirement plans funded mainly by workers themselves). Should all workers be guaranteed health care benefits and pensions?

■ The mean annual wage for computer and mathematical science occupations was $72,190 in 2007. For protective service occupations (such as firefighters and police officers), the mean annual wage was $38,750. What accounts for these differences in wages? Is there a way to ensure economic fairness for all workers?

■ These jobs are predicted to be the fastest-growing ones between 2006 and 2016:

Occupation	Predicted % Increase	Occupation	Predicted % Increase
Network systems/data communications analysts	53.4%	Computer software engineers	44.6%
Personal and home care aides	50.6%	Veterinary technologists, technicians	41%
Home health aides	48.7%	Personal financial advisors	41%

Does this chart affect your thoughts about your potential career? How so?

What Do You Think?

What is your opinion? Write a response to the Essential Question, **How can workers best meet the challenges of a changing economy?** Consider the information above, the Guiding Questions in your textbook, and the activities you have completed in your Journal and at Economics Online, including the WebQuest. See page 183 for a rubric for writing an Essential Question essay.

 Don't Forget

Your answer to this question will help you think about the Unit 3 Essential Question: **How can businesses and labor best achieve their goals?**

UNIT 3 Business and Labor

Essay Warmup

Examine the following perspectives on business and labor. The questions that follow each perspective will help you focus your thinking on the Unit 3 Essential Question, **How can businesses and labor best achieve their goals?**

> Slower labor force growth will encourage employers to [encourage] greater labor force participation among women, the elderly, and people with disabilities. . . . Rapid technological change and increased international competition spotlight the need for the workforce to be able to adapt to changing technologies and shifting product demand. Shifts in the nature of business organizations and the growing importance of knowledge-based work also favor strong non-routine [thinking] skills, such as abstract reasoning, problem-solving, communication, and collaboration.
>
> —*Lynn Karoly and Constantijn Panis, Rand Corporation*

A. What predictions do the authors make about the future makeup of the labor force?

_____

_____

B. Why is it important for both businesses and workers to be aware of potential changes in the labor market?

_____

_____

> I think the low road is where somebody thinks of only their immediate self-interest in solving their particular problem no matter what it costs to somebody else. Which means you'll have an owner of a company that'll make money . . . by destroying the community. I think you can have a labor union that . . . has a problem of protecting wages, jobs of its own members even at the expense of a regional development strategy.
>
> —*Dan Swinney, Center for Labor and Community Research, Interview, 2005*

C. According to Dan Swinney, how can self-interest become a negative quality when making economic decisions?

_____

_____

_____

_____

"Gentlemen, nothing stands in the way of a final accord except that management wants profit maximization and the union wants moola."

D. What does this cartoon suggest about the relationship between business and labor?

_____

_____

_____

E. What would you say in response to this cartoonist's point of view?

_____

_____

_____

👤 What Do You Think?

Choose one of the documents above and explain how it helps you answer the Unit 3 Essential Question, **How can businesses and labor best achieve their goals?**

_____

_____

_____

_____

_____

_____

_____

UNIT 3 Business and Labor

Essay

 How can businesses and labor best achieve their goals?

Write an essay in response to the Unit 3 Essential Question. Use your answers to the Essential Question warmup on the previous pages, your answers to the chapter Essential Questions, and what you have learned in the unit. Keep in mind that your essay should reflect your thoughtful and well-supported personal point of view. Filling in the chart below will help you structure your essay. Go to page 183 for a rubric for writing an Essential Question essay.

Thesis Statement: _____
_____

Body Paragraph 1	Body Paragraph 2	Body Paragraph 3
Main Idea _____ _____ _____ _____	**Main Idea** _____ _____ _____ _____	**Main Idea** _____ _____ _____ _____
Supporting Details 1. _____ _____ _____ 2. _____ _____ 3. _____ _____ _____	**Supporting Details** 1. _____ _____ _____ 2. _____ _____ 3. _____ _____ _____	**Supporting Details** 1. _____ _____ _____ 2. _____ _____ 3. _____ _____ _____

Conclusion: _____
_____

 Essential Question

How can you make the most of your money?

Chapter 10
Essential Question

How well do financial institutions serve our needs?

Chapter 11
Essential Question

How do your saving and investment choices affect your future?

UNIT 4 Money, Banking, and Finance

Warmup

How can you make the most of your money?

Some people say that to make money, you need to have money. To some extent, this may be true. However, it is more likely that you can make the most of your money if you analyze your savings and investment options. In Unit 4, you will study money, banking, and finance and explore possible responses to the Unit Essential Question.

Knowing the risks and benefits of buying stocks and bonds is one of the keys to wise investing.

Read the paragraph and follow the directions.

You've earned $25 by walking your neighbors' dog while they were away. Immediately, you start thinking about all the great things you could buy. However, you don't have enough money to buy everything you want, and you owe money to a friend, too.

A. Number the choices below in order from your highest to your lowest priority.

____ add to your savings account   ____ invest in your uncle's business

____ pay back your friend   ____ give to a charitable organization

____ go out to eat   ____ buy school supplies

B. Why did you decide to put the items in this order? Explain your reasoning with details from your own experiences.

_____

_____

_____

C. What are your long-term financial goals? What role does saving and investing play in how you can meet your goals?

_____

_____

CHAPTER 10 Money and Banking

Warmup

How well do financial institutions serve our needs?

A. Salt, gold, silver, and shells all have something in common. They all have been used as currency, or forms of money. Complete the chart with notes about the ways that you use money. Remember to include notes about using things other than money as currency. For example, perhaps you baby-sit in exchange for rides to your team's practices.

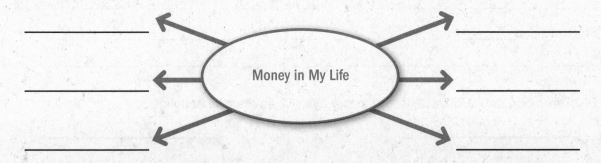

B. Think about the banking services you know. Why do people use these services? What is your opinion about these services? Complete the chart with your ideas. Some examples have been given to help you get started.

Banking Services	Why People Use Them	My Opinion
automated teller machines (ATMs)		
debit cards		
credit cards		

C. Speculate about why financial institutions do business differently today, compared to the way they did business in the past.

_____

_____

Exploration

I. Money, Utility, and Value

➡ Find Out

A. Give one example of each function of money and explain your example.

Medium of Exchange_____

_____

Unit of Account_____

_____

Store of Value_____

_____

B. In each box, write a characteristic of money and give an example or definition.

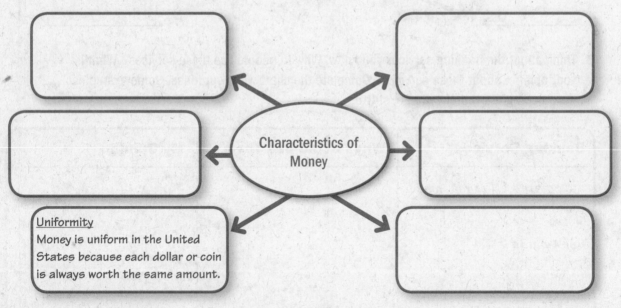

Characteristics of Money

Uniformity
Money is uniform in the United States because each dollar or coin is always worth the same amount.

👤 What Do You Think?

C. In your opinion, what commodity would best fulfill the characteristics of money if our government had to use commodity money instead of fiat money? Explain your reasoning.

_____

_____

_____

Name: _____

II. History Highlights

→ Find Out

A. The chart below lists some highlights from the history of banking. Explain how each event either created a problem—or solved a problem. Some examples are given.

Events	Problems Caused or Solved by Event
1791—Charter of the Bank of the United States	Bank brought stability to American banking by holding tax money, issuing notes backed by gold and silver, and supervising state banks.
1816—Charter of the Second Bank of the United States	
1863 and 1864—National Banking Acts	
1913—Federal Reserve Act	
1933—Federal Deposit Insurance Corporation (FDIC)	
1970s–1980s—Savings and Loan Crisis	Deregulation increased competition on S&Ls. Because they made risky loans and paid high interest rates on deposits, many S&Ls failed and many people lost money.
2000s—Sub-Prime Mortgage Crisis	

👤 What Do You Think?

B. What effect does flexibility have on the ability of financial institutions to help solve economic problems today? Support your opinion with at least one example.

_____

_____

_____

III. Making Choices About Managing Your Money

👤 What Do You Think?

For a consumer, services and fees can be important factors in deciding which financial institution to use. Read the descriptions of the four financial institutions. Which institution or institutions would you recommend to the people below, and why?

1. Convenience Commercial Bank

- Fee-based checking and savings accounts
- Loans at competitive interest rates
- Many ATMs in region; agreements to use other banks' ATMs for $1.00 additional fee
- Excellent home banking services, and automated clearing house services
- Credit cards with moderate interest rates

2. Best Bet Savings and Loan

- Free checking and savings accounts
- Loans at low interest rates, but strict loan requirements (many people turned down)
- Some ATMs in region; use of other ATMs for $2.00 fee
- Home banking services; no automated clearing house services
- Credit cards with high interest rates

3. Trust Us Savings Bank

- Offers most services that the Convenience Commercial Bank offers, but lower fees
- Loans at competitive interest rates; works with people to help them qualify for loans
- ATM at bank only; use of other ATMs for $3.00 fee
- Good home banking services; no automated clearing house services
- No credit card services

4. All for One Credit Union

- Free checking and savings accounts (open to the entire community)
- Offers the lowest loan interest rates of all the banks described here
- ATM at office only; no agreements with other institutions
- No home banking services; no automated clearing house services
- No credit card services

High School Student

_____

_____

College Student

_____

_____

Young Family

_____

_____

Two Business Owners Who Travel Often

_____

_____

IV. Taking a Closer Look at Financial Services

➔ Find Out

A. What are positive and negative features of the following financial services? Write one "pro" statement and one "con" statement for each.

"Pro" Statement	Service	"Con" Statement
A person doesn't need to carry money.	Debit Cards	Too easy to overspend when not using cash.
	Credit Cards	
	Automated Teller Machines (ATMs)	
	Home Banking or Online Banking	
	Finance Companies	
	Stored Value Cards	

👤 What Do You Think?

B. Which service do you think is most valuable to people today, and why? Which service do you think is least valuable, and why?

_____

_____

_____

C. Do you think financial institutions are prepared to meet the needs of people in the future? Why or why not?

_____

_____

Essential Question Activity

 How well do financial institutions serve our needs?

Activity

Complete this activity to answer the Essential Question.

Imagine that after many years of service, you become the manager of the bank that serves the neighborhood in which you grew up. Your responsibility to the bank is to increase its profits. However, you also want to do good works in your community. Using the worksheet on the next page, fill in the following information:

A. In the first column, write the services you will offer your customers.

B. In the second column, write how these services will benefit your neighborhood. For example, how might giving people mortgages be good for the neighborhood?

Think about which services and benefits are most likely to attract customers to your bank. Based on your ideas, write one or more advertising slogans for your bank in the third column.

Modify

Now suppose another bank opens down the block from your bank. Choose two of the following situations. Describe how each of them might cause you to modify the services you offer and how you choose to advertise.

A. The new bank offers free debit cards and electronic banking through the Internet.

B. The new bank offers low-interest mortgages—but only to borrowers who have an excellent history of paying back loans.

C. The new bank offers low-interest mortgages to poor people who want to live in their own house, but who may not be able to pay back their debt.

Services Offered	Benefits of Services	Advertising Slogans
Home mortgage loans	People in the neighborhood can buy own homes.	Let Us Help You Make Your Home Dreams Come True!

Modify

Respond to one of the situations given on the previous page.

_____

_____

_____

Respond to another situation given on the previous page.

_____

_____

Essay

 ## How well do financial institutions serve our needs?

Historically, financial institutions in the United States have both helped and hurt the economy. Today, they play a key role in managing our money supply. They also compete for customers through the services they offer. However, are they serving the needs of individuals, families, and businesses? Think about examples such as the ones below before you start writing your essay.

Financial Institutions

History	Money Supply	Services
For example: ■ The Federal Reserve was given the responsibility to protect both customers and the stability of the money supply. ■ Financial institutions were a major cause of the savings and loan and sub-prime mortgage crises. ■ Many financial institutions lack flexibility to address the needs of customers going through foreclosures.	For example: ■ A stable money supply helps make business transactions efficient. ■ People need a variety of ways to access, store, and invest money. ■ Financial institutions provide customers with many options for managing their money.	For example: ■ Loans can help people to purchase cars, homes, and businesses. ■ Electronic banking lets people bank 24-hours a day. ■ Credit cards can make shopping easier. ■ Simple and compound interest help a person's money to grow.

What Do You Think?

What is your opinion? Write a response to the Essential Question, **How well do financial institutions serve our needs?** Consider your thoughts on the examples above, the Guiding Questions in your textbook, and the activities you have completed in your Journal and at Economics Online, including the WebQuest. See page 183 for a rubric for writing an Essential Question essay.

 ### Don't Forget

Your answer to this question will help you think about the Unit 4 Essential Question: **How can you make the most of your money?**

11 Financial Markets

Warmup

 How do your saving and investment choices affect your future?

Making good saving and investment choices is tied to knowing your options. For each concept in the chart, write what you know, and then write one or two questions that you would like answered. Look for the answers to your questions as you read the chapter.

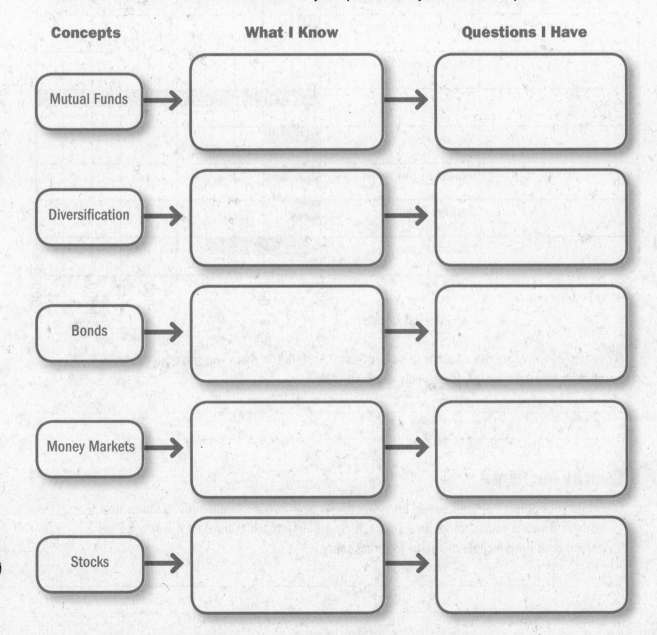

Concepts	What I Know	Questions I Have
Mutual Funds		
Diversification		
Bonds		
Money Markets		
Stocks		

CHAPTER 11 How do your saving and investment choices affect your future?

Name: _____

Exploration

I. Risks and Rewards

→ Find Out

A. Analyze how each investor has invested $10,000. Then complete the chart with the types of risk each investment holds. Possibilities include minimal risk, high risk, credit risk, liquidity risk, inflation rate risk, and time risk. Remember that investments can carry multiple risks.

Investor A ■   **Investor B** ▨

Risk Type	Investment Type						
minimal risk, liquidity risk, time risk	Certificate of Deposits						
	Savings Account						
	Hedge Fund						
	Mutual Fund						
	Individual Stocks						
	Savings Bonds						
	Personal Loan						

Amount Invested $0 $1,000 $2,000 $3,000 $4,000 $5,000

B. Are these investors risk tolerant or risk adverse? Explain the risks and possible rewards of each investor's saving and investment distribution.

_____

_____

◉ What Do You Think?

C. Would your opinion of their saving and investment distributions change if you knew that Investor B was a young person in a stable, high-paying job, while Investor A was a retired person on a fixed income? Explain your reasoning.

_____

_____

Name: _____

II. Choosing Financial Assets

👤 What Do You Think?

A. To diversify your investments, you have decided to buy three different bonds. How do you decide which bonds are best for you? Study the chart below and decide which bonds you will buy. Circle your three choices.

	Sample Coupon Rate	Sample Maturity	Possible Par Value
Savings Bond	4.78%	30 years	$50–$10,000
Treasury Bond	5%	10–30 years	$100–$5 million
Treasury Note	3%—determined at auction	2, 5, and 10 years	$100–$5 million
Treasury Bill	2.25%—determined at auction	4, 13, 26, and 52 weeks	$100–$5 million
Inflation-Indexed Bond	2%	30 years	$50–$5000
Municipal Bond	4%	20 years	Variable
Corporate Bond	3%	10 years	Variable
Junk Bond	12%	5 years	Variable

B. Explain your reasoning for your bond choices. Include what you know about the risks involved with each one.

_____

_____

_____

C. What kinds of bonds are sold on the primary markets? How might this information influence your decision about purchasing more bonds in the future?

_____

_____

_____

D. Why do you think an investor might choose a junk bond over a money market mutual fund?

_____

_____

CHAPTER 11 How do your saving and investment choices
affect your future?

Name: _____

III. Stock Talk

➡ Find Out

A. Your understanding of your options in stock purchases can make the difference between
a profit and a loss. So, it is important to know the terminology, or vocabulary, used to
discuss stocks. For each set of words in the concept web, explain how it relates to stocks.

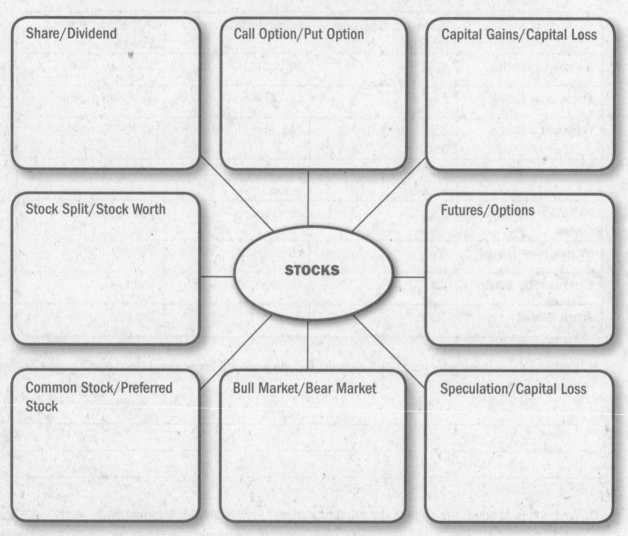

Share/Dividend

Call Option/Put Option

Capital Gains/Capital Loss

Stock Split/Stock Worth

STOCKS

Futures/Options

Common Stock/Preferred
Stock

Bull Market/Bear Market

Speculation/Capital Loss

👤 What Do You Think?

B. What risks might there be in buying stock in a company that a friend has recommended
as a "sure bet"? Explain.

_____

_____

_____

_____

CHAPTER 11 How do your saving and investment choices
affect your future?

Name: _____

IV. Speculation

👤 What Do You Think?

How important is it to take into account the general economic climate? For example, before the Great Crash of 1929, there were signs that the economy was in trouble. Recognizing these signs might have led people to make different decisions about stock purchases. Read the economic scenarios below and answer the questions that follow.

> In 2007 and 2008, the price of crude oil on the world market rose by over 100 percent. Some people attributed this rise to the law of supply and demand. They said that demand was higher all over the world, so prices rose because supply could not meet demand. Others, however, felt that the price increase was mainly caused by speculation in oil futures.

A. Given what you know about speculation and futures, explain how people could conclude that trading in oil futures could affect the price of oil.

_____

_____

> As you have learned, 2007 and 2008 was marked by a significant number of foreclosures in the housing industry. The sub-prime mortgage crisis began to affect the prime mortgage market. For example, local banks began to deny mortgage loans to people buying houses in a town if the banks felt that the houses were overpriced.

B. If a couple was willing to buy a house at a certain price (and had a good credit rating), why might a local bank deny the couple a mortgage if the bank thought the house was overpriced? Think about what banks often do with their mortgages. Also, think about what the bank might be forecasting about future house prices.

_____

_____

C. How does what you know about the volatility of the stock market affect your thinking about your future investment choices?

_____

_____

D. Return to the chart you completed in the Chapter 11 Warmup. Write brief answers to your questions on another sheet of paper. If you still have unanswered questions, look for the answers in your library or on the Internet.

CHAPTER 11 How do your saving and investment choices affect your future?

Name: _____

Essential Question Activity

 How do your saving and investment choices affect your future?

Activity

Complete this activity to answer the Essential Question.

Imagine that you have just turned 21 when you learn that a relative you have never met has died—and left you $5,000. According to the will, you must provide a plan for investing the money in the stock, mutual fund, and bond markets that will meet the financial needs you expect to have when you are 30 years old. Using the worksheet on the next page, answer the following questions.

A. What career path do you expect to be following when you are 30? How much money do you expect to be making?

B. What financial responsibilities will you have when you are 30? Will you have student loans to pay? Will you have a family to support? Will you own a house? Will you have expensive interests such as travel or collecting?

C. Based on your income and your responsibilities, how much money will you need from your investments? Will you depend on that income, or can you risk losing some of it?

Use your answers to these questions about your financial needs to help you make your investment plan. Remember to diversify between relatively safe and relatively high-return investments, depending on your predicted needs.

Modify

Suppose that when you are 30, you decide to review your investments. Look at the situations below. Briefly describe how each of them might cause you to change your investment plan.

A. Interest rates are very high.

B. There is a bull market with low interest rates.

C. The stock market is doing well, but many economists are predicting a bleak future in the next year for stocks.

D. You are about to buy a house—and become the parent of twins.

CHAPTER 11 How do your saving and investment choices affect your future?

Name: _____

A. Career? Salary?	C. Financial Needs?
B. Responsibilities?	

Complete the outline below with your financial plan for $5,000 invested over a period of nine years. List how much you plan to invest in each category. Then use colored pencils or markers to create a circle graph illustrating your plan. Remember to convert your dollar investment amounts to percentages for the graph.

■ Stock market investments:

_____ Income stock

_____ Growth stock

_____ Other stock

■ Mutual fund investments:

_____

_____

■ Bond market investments:

_____ Savings bonds

_____ Treasury bonds, bills, and notes

_____ Municipal bonds

_____ Corporate bonds

_____ Junk bonds

_____ TOTAL

Note: Your investment amounts must total $5,000.

Note: Your percentages must total 100%.

Explain why this plan will meet your needs as you defined them in your chart above.

_____

_____

_____

_____

Modify

Respond to each of the situations given on the previous page. Use another sheet of paper.

CHAPTER 11 How do your saving and investment choices affect your future?

Name: _____

Essay

How do your saving and investment choices affect your future?

Planning—or not planning—your saving and investment choices can greatly affect your future. Finding the balance between more risk and less risk, is an ongoing process. As your needs change, your plan must also change. Consider these possible situations.

- After college, you have a large debt to repay. As a graduation gift, you received $1,000 dollars from your parents to help you get started. You decide to use the money to . . .

- When you are in your late twenties, a close friend decides to open a restaurant. Your friend asks you to invest the $10,000 from your retirement account in this venture. You value the friendship and decide to . . .

- Your 80-year-old mother has had some health problems recently. Your father is having trouble taking care of her. To fund the cost of a home health aide, you advise them to . . .

- The stock market has taken a dive and you are glad that you diversified your portfolio. You are now 55 years old and your stockbroker is urging you to take advantage of the lower prices and buy more stocks. You mull it over and decide to . . .

- You have owned your own home for several years and would like to renovate the kitchen. After looking at the interest rates for loans versus the amount you are earning in a money market account, you decide to . . .

How would what you have learned in this chapter help you to make these decisions?

What Do You Think?

What is your opinion? Write a response to the Essential Question, **How do your saving and investment choices affect your future?** Consider your thoughts on the situations above, the Guiding Questions in your textbook, and the activities you have completed in your Journal and at Economics Online, including the WebQuest. See page 183 for a rubric for writing an Essential Question essay.

Don't Forget

Your answer to this question will help you think about the Unit 4 Essential Question: **How can you make the most of your money?**

UNIT 4 Money, Banking, and Finance

Essay Warmup

Examine the following perspectives on money, banking, and finance. The questions that follow each perspective will help you focus your thinking on the Unit 4 Essential Question, **How can you make the most of your money?**

> Legend has it that Albert Einstein once called compound interest the most powerful force in the universe. Compound interest is the engine that can turn even meager savings into a nice nest egg over time. Inattention to debt puts you on the wrong side of that equation. You spend dollars that could be put to work making you wealthy. You want to be on the right side—the side that uses debt to make money but avoids debt when it hurts. . . . Stop watching your money go up in smoke.
>
> —*Mary Dalrymple,* Habits for Wealth: Dump Your Debt Habit

A. What do you think the author means by saying, "You want to be on . . . the side that uses debt to make money but avoids debt when it hurts?"_____

_____

B. How important do you think compound interest is to successful investing? Provide two reasons in support of your opinion._____

_____

> I don't know what the stock market will do tomorrow. (And, let me be equally clear, neither does anyone else.) Bad things may happen tomorrow. Certainly, bad things will happen on some days. . . . You get a great return [from stocks] by noticing that the day-to-day price of the market doesn't have much to do with the real long-term value of the best companies within that market. You get an even better return than the market averages by never mixing up three very important facts: Extreme stock market pessimism is great for buyers, extreme exuberance is great for sellers . . . and stocks are long-term investments.
>
> —*John Casper,* Lessons Learned

C. Do you agree with the author that "stocks are long-term investments"? Why or why not?

_____

_____

D. What does this cartoon suggest about saving and investing?

_____

_____

_____

E. What would you say in response to this cartoonist's point of view?

_____

_____

_____

👤 What Do You Think?

Choose one of the documents above and explain how it helps you answer the
Unit 4 Essential Question, **How can you make the most of your money?**

_____

_____

_____

_____

_____

_____

_____

_____

UNIT 4 Money, Banking, and Finance

Essay

 How can you make the most of your money?

Write an essay in response to the Unit 4 Essential Question. Use your answers to the Essential Question warmup on the previous pages, your answers to the chapter Essential Questions, and what you have learned in the unit. Keep in mind that your essay should reflect your thoughtful and well-supported personal point of view. Filling in the chart below will help you structure your essay. Go to page 183 for a rubric for writing an Essential Question essay.

Thesis Statement: _____

_____

Body Paragraph 1	Body Paragraph 2	Body Paragraph 3
Main Idea	**Main Idea**	**Main Idea**
_____ _____ _____ _____	_____ _____ _____ _____	_____ _____ _____ _____
Supporting Details	**Supporting Details**	**Supporting Details**
1. _____ _____	1. _____ _____	1. _____ _____
2. _____ _____	2. _____ _____	2. _____ _____
3. _____ _____	3. _____ _____	3. _____ _____

Conclusion: _____

_____

Unit 5

Measuring Economic Performance

Essential Question

Why does it matter how the economy is doing?

Chapter 12
Essential Question

How do we know if the economy is healthy?

Chapter 13
Essential Question

How much can we reduce unemployment, inflation, and poverty?

UNIT 5 Measuring Economic Performance

Job Opportunities

Warmup

Why does it matter how the economy is doing?

Think about it: the economy is our national budget. It shows how well we are working, saving, and investing. The economy also indicates our failures in terms of unemployment, inflation, and poverty. In Unit 5, you will study how economists measure the health of the economy and explore possible responses to the Unit Essential Question.

Unemployment represents both a challenge and an opportunity.

Brainstorm ways in which the national economy affects areas of your life. A few topics are given below, but you may add your own ideas to the web.

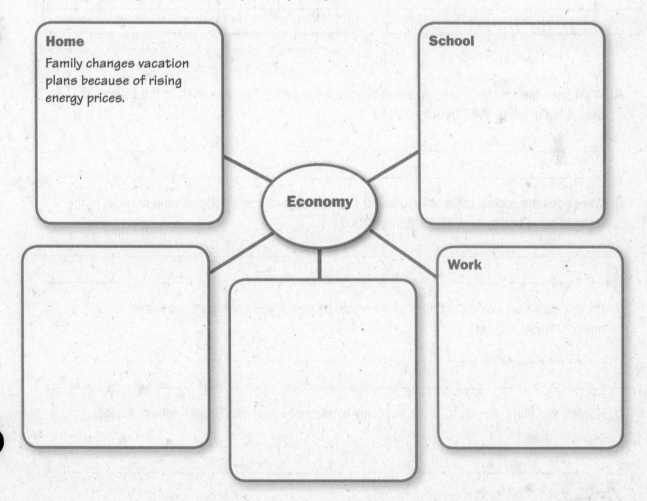

Home
Family changes vacation plans because of rising energy prices.

School

Economy

Work

CHAPTER 12 Gross Domestic Product and Growth

Warmup

How do we know if the economy is healthy?

How much money do you have in your wallet? What kinds of decisions do you make based on that information? Study the following tables and answer the questions about how economic data affects economic policy.

Gross Domestic Product for the United States: TOTAL (millions of current dollars)										
1997	1998	1999	2000	2001	2002	2003	2004	2005	2006	2007
8,237,994	8,679,657	9,201,138	9,749,103	10,058,168	10,398,402	10,886,172	11,607,041	12,346,87	13,119,938	13,743,021

Gross Domestic Product for the United States: EDUCATIONAL SERVICES (millions of current dollars)										
1997	1998	1999	2000	2001	2002	2003	2004	2005	2006	2007
62,240	67,634	72,774	79,239	85,094	93,268	100,096	108,296	113,940	120,946	129,411

Source: Bureau of Economic Analysis, U.S. Department of Commerce

A. What does the first table tell you about the Gross Domestic Product (GDP) in the United States in the years 1997 through 2007?

_____

_____

B. What does the second table tell you about the GDP as it relates to educational services in the United States in the years 1997 through 2007?

_____

_____

C. Do you think that just these tables alone would be useful in determining economic policy? Why or why not?

_____

_____

D. How do you think the health of the economy is related to your own opportunities? Explain.

_____

_____

Exploration

I. Measures of Growth

➔ Find Out

A. Complete the chart below with what you know about different economic indicators.
Explain why economists and government policy makers might find each measure useful.

Gross National Product =	GDP plus . . .	income earned outside the U.S. by U.S. firms and citizens minus . . .	income earned by foreign firms and foreign citizens located in the U.S.
Usefulness of Measure: This measure allows economists and policy makers to determine all income earned by U.S. citizens and firms. This might help them determine the appropriate level of taxes on income.			
National Income =			
Usefulness of Measure:			
Disposable Personal Income =			
Usefulness of Measure:			
Personal Income =			
Usefulness of Measure:			
Net National Product =			
Usefulness of Measure:			

👤 What Do You Think?

B. GDP and other economic indicators do not measure all aspects of the economy. List
three other ways that you think could be used to help measure the economy's health.
Then explain how your indicators would do this.

_____

_____

_____

II. Push and Pull

→ Find Out

Aggregate supply and demand for goods and services affect the prices that you pay at stores, but they are also a measure of the general health of the economy.

A. Use the graph at right to help you complete the statements below.

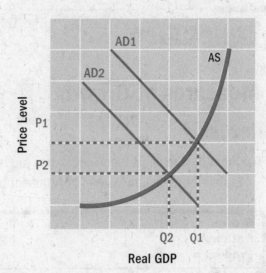

| | | | | | | |
| 1. If the average of all prices in the economy increases . . . | → | . . . then demand _____ _____ |

| 2. If aggregate demand increases . . . | → | . . . then GDP _____ _____ |

| 3. If the average of all prices in the economy decreases . . . | → | . . . then demand _____ _____ |

| 4. If prices decrease . . . | → | . . . then business _____ _____ |

👤 What Do You Think?

B. What one factor do you think influences aggregate demand the most: How people feel about the economy? Wages? Another factor? Explain.

_____

_____

_____

III. Ups and Downs

⊙ Find Out

A. Read each description. Label the business cycle graph with the number of the scenario that describes an expansion, a peak, a contraction, or a trough.

1. Unemployment is high, interest rates are high, and many businesses are not investing, but real GDP is no longer falling.

2. Business production is down and unemployment is rising. Real GDP has been falling in recent months.

3. Unemployment has been dropping and businesses are doing well. Real GDP is experiencing a long-term increase.

4. Business is doing well and unemployment is low, but real GDP is no longer rising.

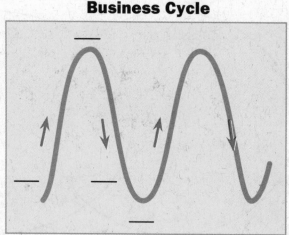

Business Cycle

👤 What Do You Think?

B. Do you think consumer confidence plays a major role or a minor one in the business cycle? Explain.

_____

_____

C. At the beginning of the Great Depression, how might President Herbert Hoover have changed his actions if information from the Conference Board had been available to him?

_____

_____

D. Suppose that the leading economic indicators, such as stock prices and interest rates, all show positive news about the national economy. However, you have been looking for a summer job for over a month without any luck. What do you think are the possible economic reasons that might explain your lack of success?

_____

_____

_____

Name: _____

IV. Economic Growth

→ Find Out

A. How do the factors shown in the chart below affect each other and influence economic growth? Fill in the areas of the circles with your ideas. Then, in the box, explain how these factors influence economic growth.

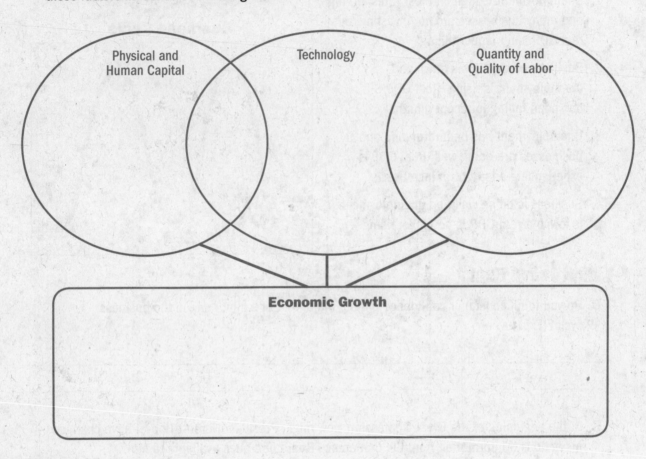

Physical and Human Capital

Technology

Quantity and Quality of Labor

Economic Growth

👤 What Do You Think?

B. Think about quality of life issues, such as the environment and human happiness. Do you think increasing economic growth will always result in a better quality of life? Why or why not?

_____

_____

C. If technology is the key to economic growth, do you think American students need more education and training in technology-related areas? Explain.

_____

_____

_____

Essential Question Activity

 ## How do we know if the economy is healthy?

Activity

Complete this activity to answer the Essential Question.

Work in groups to gather information to take the current pulse of the American economy. Track your data over a three-year period. Use the worksheet on the next page to gather the following information:

A. What trend does the real Gross Domestic Product of the United States reveal?

B. Was there an unemployment rate contraction phase? If so, how long did it last?

C. At what point during these three years did the rate of inflation peak?

Modify

Once you have collected your information, provide a forecast for the next three months (quarter). Select one of the economic indicators used.

A. In which phase of the business cycle does the graph end? Do you anticipate a change? If so, to which phase?

B. Determine the pattern that this indicator has followed over the past three years. Indicate what you think it might do within the next quarter.

U.S. Economic Indicators: _____ through _____

Economic Indicator	Year 1	Year 2	Year 3
Gross Domestic Product			
Unemployment Rate			
Inflation Rate			

Use your completed chart above to create a graph showing the data from all three indicators and then answer the questions that follow.

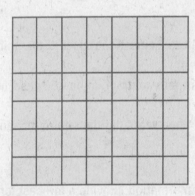

A. What trend does the real GDP of the United States reveal?

_____

_____

B. Was there an unemployment rate contraction phase? If so, how long did it last?

_____

_____

C. At what point during these three years did the inflation rate peak? What do these indicators tell us about current activity in the U.S. economy? What other indicators might also be helpful in examining the economy?

_____

_____

_____

_____

Modify

Choose one of the economic indicators used in the activity, and then respond to both A and B on the previous page. Use a separate sheet of paper.

Essay

How do we know if the economy is healthy?

Economists use many different measures to analyze the economy. As you have learned, these measures directly relate to your life. Understanding these measures can help you make decisions about your participation in the economy. Consider these statistics:

- In 2006, the percentage of children under 18 living in poverty was 18.3 percent. In the District of Columbia, that percentage rose to 32.6 percent for the same year. –*U.S. Census Bureau*

- In 2007, the per capita real GDP was about $38,020 in the United States. –*U.S. Bureau of Economic Analysis*

- In 2006, the percentage of people spending 30 percent or more of their income on their mortgage was approximately 36.9 percent. –*U.S. Census Bureau*

- There was a significant slowing of real economic growth between 2006 and 2007. It changed from 3.1 percent in 2006 to 2.0 percent in 2007. –*U.S. Bureau of Economic Analysis*

- In the first quarter of 2008, the real GDP was calculated to be growing at an annual rate of 1 percent. –*U.S. Bureau of Economic Analysis*

- The unemployment rate in 2008 rose in the first 6 months of the year from 4.9 to 5.5 percent. –*U.S. Bureau of Labor Statistics*

How do the statistics above compare to the current economic situation? How do these economic indicators reflect people's quality of life?

What Do You Think?

What is your opinion? Write a response to the Essential Question, **How do we know if the economy is healthy?** Consider the statistics above, the Guiding Questions in your textbook, and the activities you have completed in your Journal and at Economics Online, including the WebQuest. See page 183 for a rubric for writing an Essential Question essay.

 Don't Forget

Your answer to this question will help you think about the Unit 5 Essential Question: **Why does it matter how the economy is doing?**

CHAPTER 13 Economic Challenges

Warmup

How much can we reduce unemployment, inflation, and poverty?

Think about possible solutions for unemployment, inflation, and poverty. A decision tree can help you visualize the consequences of your proposed solutions. For example, how might higher wages reduce poverty, but increase inflation? Complete the decision tree with your ideas about ways to solve these economic challenges. Include positive and negative consequences your ideas might have. One path has been started for you as an example. Add boxes or change connections as needed.

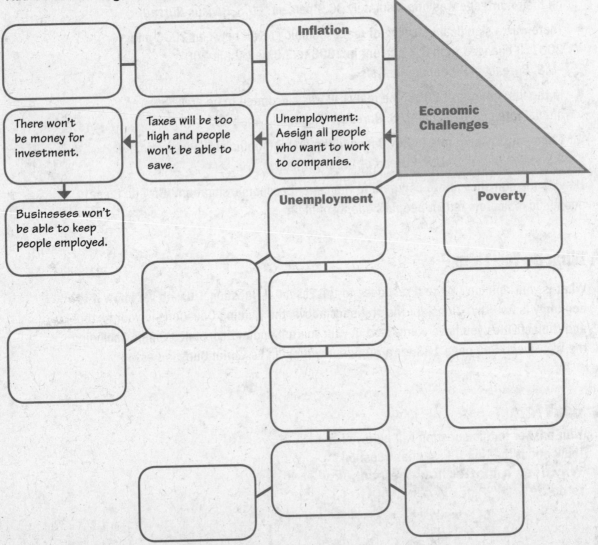

CHAPTER 13 How much can we reduce unemployment, inflation, and poverty?

Name: _____

Exploration

I. Causes of Unemployment

→ Find Out

A. Explain how each category of unemployment affects the economy.

Frictional	E
Seasonal	C O N O M Y
Structural	
Cyclical	

B. Describe an example of structural employment that has affected your community. What solutions were implemented?

_____

_____

_____

👤 What Do You Think?

C. How do you think that a worker affected by seasonal unemployment might increase his or her income?

_____

_____

D. What do you think is the best way to keep unemployment low? Explain.

_____

_____

CHAPTER 13 How much can we reduce unemployment, inflation, and poverty?

Name: _____

II. The Cost of Being a Consumer

➔ Find Out

A. The Consumer Price Index (CPI) shows how much the prices of necessary items are changing. For example, in 2007 the CPI for all items was 4.1 percent. Research CPI rates at www.bls.gov/cpi to complete the chart below.

CPI Market Basket Items: Percent of Price Increase

	2007	Last Year	Last Month
All Items	4.1		
Food and Drink	4.8		
Housing	3.0		
Apparel	-0.3		
Transportation	8.3		
Medical Care	5.2		
Recreation and Entertainment	0.8		
Education and Communication	3.0		
Other Goods and Services	3.3		

What Do You Think?

B. Now, analyze your completed chart. In your opinion, is inflation worse now than it was in 2007? Why or why not?

_____

_____

_____

C. Suppose you had to plan your family's budget for next year. How would you use this completed chart to help you make your budget?

_____

_____

D. You read about safety net programs in Chapter 3. Based on your completed chart, do you think the state or local government should provide more help to families who are poor when inflation increases? Why or why not?

_____

_____

_____

CHAPTER 13 How much can we reduce unemployment, inflation, and poverty?

Name: _____

III. Ins and Outs of Inflation

Find Out

A. Give at least one example of each cause of inflation. Then, write examples of how the government might act to address each effect of inflation.

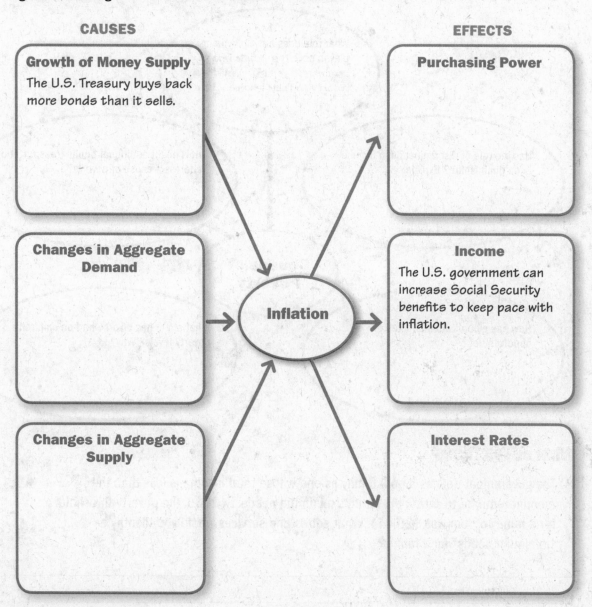

CAUSES

Growth of Money Supply
The U.S. Treasury buys back more bonds than it sells.

Changes in Aggregate Demand

Changes in Aggregate Supply

Inflation

EFFECTS

Purchasing Power

Income
The U.S. government can increase Social Security benefits to keep pace with inflation.

Interest Rates

What Do You Think?

B. Do you think that the government should try to control all aspects of inflation? Why or why not?

_____

_____

_____

CHAPTER 13 How much can we reduce unemployment, inflation, and poverty?

Name: _____

IV. Poverty

➡️ Find Out

A. In the concept web, answer the questions about some causes of poverty and how they affect people.

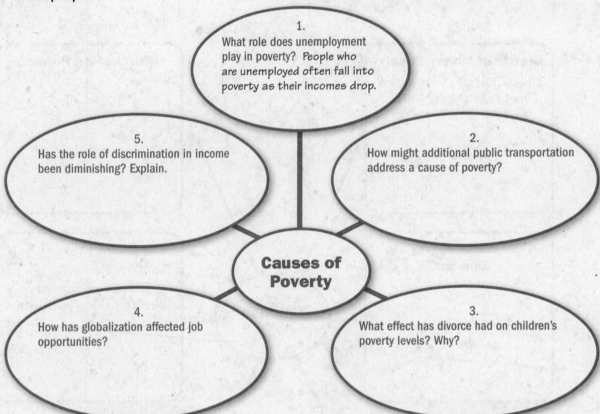

Causes of Poverty

1. What role does unemployment play in poverty? People who are unemployed often fall into poverty as their incomes drop.

5. Has the role of discrimination in income been diminishing? Explain.

2. How might additional public transportation address a cause of poverty?

4. How has globalization affected job opportunities?

3. What effect has divorce had on children's poverty levels? Why?

👤 What Do You Think?

B. The government defines a poor family as one whose total income is less than the amount required to satisfy the family's minimum needs. In 2006, the poverty threshold for a family of four was $20,444. What goods and services would you identify as "minimum needs" for a family?

_____

_____

C. In your area, estimate how much income it would take to meet those minimum needs. In your view, is the 2006 poverty threshold a reasonable number? Why or why not?

_____

_____

_____

_____

CHAPTER 13 How much can we reduce unemployment, inflation, and poverty?

Name: _____

V. Poverty Solutions

→ Find Out

A. Draw Lorenz Curves for the following data from the U.S. Census Bureau and then answer the questions.

Florida Estimates 2006
Lowest fifth: 3.6
Second fifth: 8.9
Third fifth: 14.6
Fourth fifth: 22.4
Highest fifth: 50.5

Wisconsin Estimates 2006
Lowest fifth: 4.1
Second fifth: 10.0
Third fifth: 16.0
Fourth fifth: 23.6
Highest fifth: 46.3

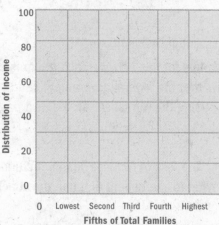

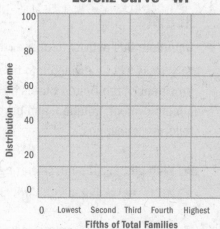

B. Compare these Lorenz Curves with the national Lorenz Curve in your textbook. What similarities and differences do you note?

_____

_____

👤 What Do You Think?

C. In general, the income gap between rich and poor has been growing since 1977. What do you think government should do, if anything, to close this gap? Explain.

_____

_____

_____

D. In your opinion, what is the most important economic challenge facing the United States today? Provide support for your response.

_____

_____

_____

CHAPTER 13 How much can we reduce unemployment, inflation, and poverty?

Name: _____

Essential Question Activity

How much can we reduce unemployment, inflation, and poverty?

Activity

Complete this activity to answer the Essential Question.

Your class will be divided into three groups for this activity. Each group is advising the President of the United States on ways that the federal government can help reduce unemployment, inflation, and poverty. Using the worksheet on the next page, answer the following questions:

A. With globalization accelerating, and the loss of America's manufacturing base, what can we do to reduce unemployment? What is one benefit and one drawback of your plan?

B. What strategy or strategies would you recommend to reduce inflation? What is one benefit and one drawback of your plan?

C. What strategy or strategies would you recommend to reduce poverty? What is one benefit and one drawback of your plan?

Modify

Present your group's ideas to the class. As a class, discuss the suggestions from all the groups:

A. What are the best ideas for reducing unemployment? What are the best ideas for controlling inflation? What are the best ideas for reducing poverty?

B. Do any of these ideas and goals conflict with each other? How? (For example, cutting taxes without reducing government spending could trigger inflation. Cutting taxes and cutting spending on entitlement programs could put more children below the poverty level.)

C. How can these conflicts best be resolved?

D. At the conclusion of your discussion, identify which steps you think would be most effective and most acceptable to the majority of the population.

CHAPTER 13 How much can we reduce unemployment, inflation, and poverty?

Name: _____

Topic	Proposed Plans	Benefits	Drawbacks
Unemployment			
Inflation			
Poverty			

Modify

Respond to the questions on the previous page. Use another sheet of paper if necessary.

A. _____

_____

B. _____

_____

C. _____

_____

D. _____

_____

CHAPTER 13 How much can we reduce unemployment, inflation, and poverty?

Name: _____

Essay

How much can we reduce unemployment, inflation, and poverty?

Unemployment, inflation, and poverty are economic problems that affect most people, whether they live in the United States or in other countries. Solutions to these problems are hard to find, since so many solutions have unintended or undesirable consequences. Consider the statements below:

"For every year of education, wages increase by a worldwide average of 10 percent."
—www.care.org

"Inflation is never ultimately tamed. It only becomes subdued."
—Alan Greenspan, former Chairman of the U.S. Federal Reserve Board

Unemployment Inflation Poverty

"It's a recession when your neighbor loses his {or her} job; it's a depression when you lose your own."
—Harry S Truman, 33rd President of the United States

"Poverty devastates families, communities and nations. It causes instability and political unrest and fuels conflict."
—Kofi Annan, former Secretary-General of the United Nations

What Do You Think?

What is your opinion? Write a response to the Essential Question, **How much can we reduce unemployment, inflation, and poverty?** Consider the quotes above, the Guiding Questions in your textbook, and the activities you have completed in your Journal and at Economics Online, including the WebQuest. See page 183 for a rubric for writing an Essential Question essay.

Don't Forget

Your answer to this question will help you think about the Unit 5 Essential Question: **Why does it matter how the economy is doing?**

UNIT 5 Measuring Economic Performance

Essay Warmup

Examine the following opinions on GDP and economic challenges facing the United States. The questions that follow each opinion will help you focus your thinking on the Unit 5 Essential Question, **Why does it matter how the economy is doing?**

> Economists readily concede that GDP is not a one-number-fits-all view of what's going on. Some suggest changes to make it more useful and more accurate. . . . 'What we need to end up with is two separate accounts [of the economy]—a market price account and a quality of life account,' says Rob Atkinson, an economist in Washington. . . . 'It is an opportunity to think more accurately about our economic well-being.'
>
> —*Mark Trumbull, "Does GDP Really Capture Economic Health?"*
> Christian Science Monitor, *March 12, 2008*

A. How could having a "quality of life account" help people to better understand how the economy is doing?

_____

_____

> The U.S. economy is taking hits from all directions, or that's how it seems to many Americans. . . . Home foreclosures are multiplying. People with houses can't sell them. Home prices and sales dropped dramatically in January, and there's no sign of improvement soon. Banks no longer provide easy credit. Stock-market investments are on a roller-coaster ride. Pay checks don't buy as much today as yesterday. . . . Americans want to know what will turn the economy around. They want help and answers—from Congress and the president.
>
> —Miami Herald, *February 29, 2008*

B. Why does this newspaper think that Americans want help from Congress and the President?

_____

_____

_____

_____

_____

"I DON'T UNDERSTAND HOW HIGH INTEREST RATES AND THE NATIONAL DEFICIT AFFECT MY ALLOWANCE."

C. What does this cartoon say about how people react if the economy is not doing well?

_____

_____

_____

D. What do you think is this cartoonist's point of view on the economy? Explain.

_____

_____

_____

What Do You Think?

Choose one of the documents above and explain how it helps you answer the Unit 5 Essential Question, **Why does it matter how the economy is doing?**

_____

_____

_____

_____

_____

_____

_____

_____

UNIT 5 Measuring Economic Performance

Essay

 Why does it matter how the economy is doing?

Write an essay in response to the Unit 5 Essential Question. Use your answers to the Essential Question warmup on the previous pages, your answers to the chapter Essential Questions, and what you have learned in the unit. Keep in mind that your essay should reflect your thoughtful and well-supported personal point of view. Filling in the chart below will help you structure your essay. Go to page 183 for a rubric for writing an Essential Question essay.

Thesis Statement: _____

_____

Body Paragraph 1	Body Paragraph 2	Body Paragraph 3
Main Idea	**Main Idea**	**Main Idea**
_____ _____ _____ _____	_____ _____ _____ _____	_____ _____ _____ _____
Supporting Details	**Supporting Details**	**Supporting Details**
1. _____ _____	1. _____ _____	1. _____ _____
2. _____ _____ _____	2. _____ _____ _____	2. _____ _____ _____
3. _____ _____ _____	3. _____ _____ _____	3. _____ _____ _____

Conclusion: _____

_____

Unit 6

Government and the Economy

Essential Question

What is the proper role of government in the economy?

Chapter 14
Essential Question

How can taxation meet the needs of government and the people?

Chapter 15
Essential Question

How effective is fiscal policy as an economic tool?

Chapter 16
Essential Question

How effective is monetary policy as an economic tool?

Name: _____

Warmup

What is the proper role of government in the economy?

The government plays a large role in the economy by collecting taxes, spending that money on public services, and by controlling the amount of money available. In Unit 6, you will learn about government taxes, spending, and fiscal and monetary policy, and explore possible responses to the Unit Essential Question.

Tax policies can encourage—or discourage—private investment in areas such as solar power.

A. Think about various government activities, and then complete the chart below.

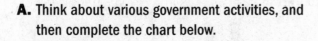

Government Activity	What do you think is government's goal?	Whom does it help/Who pays less?	Whom does it hurt/Who pays more?
Your state will collect no sales tax for 3 days on large consumer purchases.	Goal is to encourage more consumer spending.	Consumers pay less; businesses sell more.	State collects less sales tax; may have to increase other taxes later.
Your town's school committee increases fees for taking part in sports and other school activities.			
Your state decides to build a bigger bridge for an area now served by a small one.			
The federal government announces a tax rebate for people who install energy-saving devices at home.			

B. Do you think the government should play a larger or smaller role in the economy than it does? Explain.

_____

_____

CHAPTER 14 Taxes and Government Spending

Warmup

How can taxation meet the needs of government and the people?

A. The circle graphs below represent weekly paychecks. Suppose that the one on the left is for $100 per week for work at a part-time job during high school. The one on the right is for a full-time job after graduating from college, for $1,000 per week. How much of each paycheck are you willing to pay for government services? Draw a pie slice to show the percentage. Then list the actual percentage and dollar amount. An example is given.

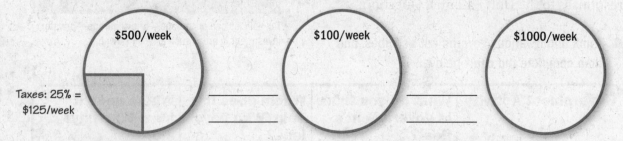

$500/week

Taxes: 25% = $125/week

$100/week

$1000/week

Now do the same steps for the following examples. The circle on the left represents income from a pension and Social Security for a retired elderly couple of $600 per week. The one on the right represents an income of $6,000 per week for a professional couple.

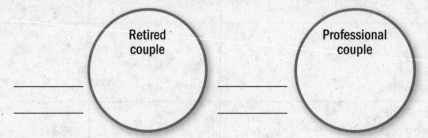

Retired couple

Professional couple

B. Did you choose the same percentage for each example? Why or why not?

_____

_____

C. What do you think are the most important services the government provides? Would you be willing to pay more in taxes to ensure that government could continue to provide these services? Why or why not?

_____

_____

CHAPTER 14 How can taxation meet the needs of
government and the people?

Name: _____

Exploration

I. Tax Fundamentals

➡ Find Out

A. Study the chart below to see how different tax structures affect the proportion of income
paid in taxes. Then, make a graph for each state using the information from the chart.
Label each state as having a proportional, regressive, or progressive tax structure.

State A			State B			State C	
Yearly Income	Income Tax Rate		Yearly Income	Income Tax Rate		Yearly Income	Sales Tax* (percent of income paid for a 5% tax on food)
$20,000	0%		$20,000	5%		$20,000	1.5%
$50,000	5%		$50,000	5%		$50,000	0.6%
$100,000	10%		$100,000	5%		$100,000	0.3%
$150,000	15%		$150,000	5%		$150,000	0.2%

Note: The amount spent on food equals $6,000 for each income level.

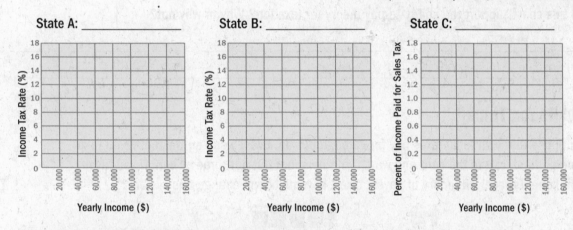

State A: _____ State B: _____ State C: _____

B. Analyze the following situations. Then, identify the tax base as Individual Income (**I**),
Corporate Income (**C**), Property (**P**), or Sales (**S**). Also, identify the tax structure as
Progressive (**Pr**), Proportional/Flat (**F**), or Regressive (**R**).

	Tax Base	Tax Structure
All retail chains pay a 10% state tax on profits each year.		
All homeowners in Springfield pay a tax of 5% per $1,000, based on the value of their homes.		
A teacher pays 8% state income tax on his salary of $40,000; a professor pays 12% on her salary of $90,000.		
A couple pays a 2.5% tax when they buy a new refrigerator.		

CHAPTER 14 How can taxation meet the needs of government and the people?

Name: _____

II. Who Should Pay? How Much Should They Pay?

⊙ Find Out

A. Explain why consumers end up paying most of an added tax on a product with a predictable, inelastic demand (such as gasoline) while companies often pay most of an added tax on a product with a variable, elastic demand (such as luxury watches).

_____

_____

_____

B. Complete the chart below.

Person	Income/Yr.	Tax Rate	Tax Paid	Remaining Income to Spend
A	$20,000	5%	$1,000	$19,000
B	$50,000	15%		
C	$100,000	30%		
D	$500,000	40%		

Does this chart support the ability-to-pay theory for taxation? Why or why not?

_____

_____

⊙ What Do You Think?

C. Suppose that your local taxes pay for garbage pickup. Every week on trash day, you take one garbage can to the curb and watch your neighbor put out three or four. If you favor the benefits-received theory of paying taxes, how might you change this system?

_____

_____

_____

D. Do you think government should use incentives, such as tax credits, to encourage certain activities (for example, energy efficiency)? Explain.

_____

_____

_____

CHAPTER 14 How can taxation meet the needs of
government and the people?

Name: _____

III. A Closer Look at Federal Taxes

→ Find Out

A. Provide one example of each of the following types of taxes:

Import tax _____   Gift tax _____

Estate tax _____   Social insurance tax _____

B. Review the graph and answer the questions below.

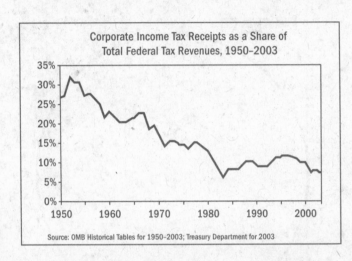

Corporate Income Tax Receipts as a Share of
Total Federal Tax Revenues, 1950–2003

Source: OMB Historical Tables for 1950–2003; Treasury Department for 2003

Why do you think corporate income taxes have
fallen since the 1950s?

_____

_____

_____

Who do you think has paid a larger share of
taxes since the 1950s?

_____

_____

_____

Why would some people today say that this trend is good for the economy?

_____

_____

_____

👤 What Do You Think?

C. Economists suggest that a "good tax" is simple, efficient, certain, and equitable (fair).
What kind of a tax do you think is the best one to use to provide for the needs of
government and the people? Explain.

_____

_____

_____

_____

_____

CHAPTER 14 How can taxation meet the needs of
government and the people?

Name: _____

IV. Analyzing Federal Spending

➔ Find Out

A. Suppose that your new job paid you $1,000 a week, or $52,000 per year. You get your
first weekly paycheck and see that $250 has been withheld from your check for federal
taxes. Divide Pie Chart B with the amount you wish you could pay each year for the
listed programs in Pie Chart A. Include the percentage and total yearly amount for each
area—assume that you pay $250 in taxes each week for one year. Also, identify each
area as *M* for mandatory spending or *D* for discretionary spending.

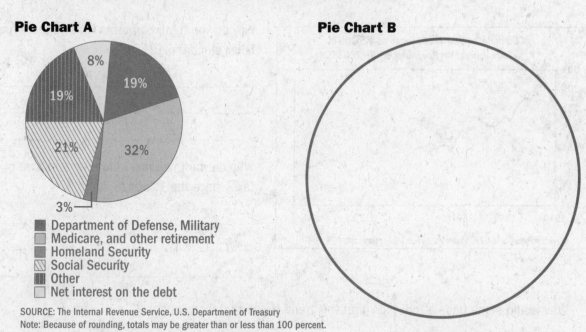

Pie Chart A

- Department of Defense, Military
- Medicare, and other retirement
- Homeland Security
- Social Security
- Other
- Net interest on the debt

Pie Chart B

SOURCE: The Internal Revenue Service, U.S. Department of Treasury
Note: Because of rounding, totals may be greater than or less than 100 percent.

B. Explain your reasons for increasing and/or decreasing any of the percentages in Pie
Chart B compared to Pie Chart A. (If you kept Pie Chart B's percentages all the same as
in Pie Chart A, explain why you had no changes.)

_____

_____

_____

👤 What Do You Think?

C. The U.S. Food Stamp Program helps people who are poor get enough food to eat. On
average, people who qualify receive about $100 worth of food stamps per month. Do
you think this program is an effective way to meet the food needs of people? Explain.

_____

_____

_____

Name: _____

V. A Closer Look at State and Local Taxes and Spending

→ Find Out

A. Summarize why separating operating and capital budgets makes it easier to balance a
state budget compared to the federal budget.

_____

_____

_____

B. Provide two or more examples from your state or local government for each type of spending.

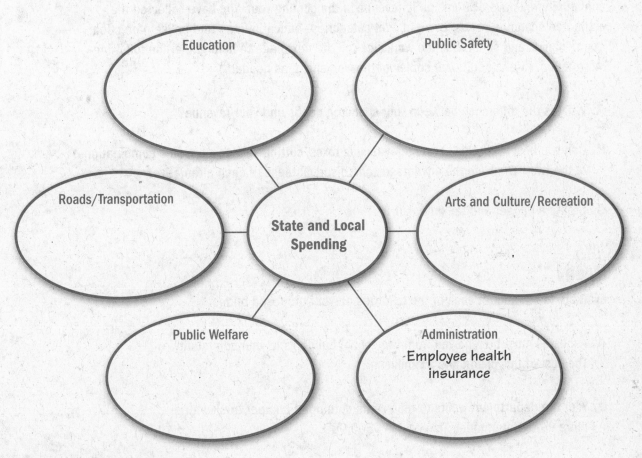

Education

Public Safety

Roads/Transportation

**State and Local
Spending**

Arts and Culture/Recreation

Public Welfare

Administration
-Employee health
insurance

● What Do You Think?

C. How valuable are government services to your community (for public education, police,
fire, and so on)? To your family? To you? Explain.

_____

_____

CHAPTER 14 How can taxation meet the needs of
government and the people?

Name: _____

Essential Question Activity

How can taxation meet the needs of government and the people?

Activity

Complete this activity to answer the Essential Question.

Suppose that you are on the council of your local community. At current tax rates, the community will have $59 million in revenue in the coming year. You have collected the estimated spending needs for all budget categories—education, fire and police protection, maintenance, and so on. Use the worksheet on the next page to help gather the following information. (Make additional copies of the worksheet, as needed.)

A. What is the difference between your spending needs and your revenue?

B. Can you best meet this shortage by raising taxes, cutting services, or some combination of the two? What are the advantages and disadvantages of each alternative?

C. Create a budget and tax proposal.

Modify

Evaluate the impact of each of the following on your proposed budget.

A. Asbestos must be removed from two school buildings in your community. The cost of this cleanup is $3 million.

B. Your fire department wants to replace its outmoded pumper truck with a more up-to-date model. This cost is $500,000.

C. You are having trouble hiring road maintenance workers because neighboring communities pay higher wages. In order to compete, you have to raise wages and benefits a total of $750,000.

CHAPTER 14 How can taxation meet the needs of
government and the people?

Name: _____

Tax Revenues—Income			Budget Requests—Spending		
Type of Tax	Projected Income (in millions of $)	Changed Amount (or same)	Department/ Area	Amount Requested (in millions of $)	Changed Amount (or same)
Property	$20.7		Education	$24.5	
State/Federal Aid*	$21.5*	$21.5*	Police & Fire	$5	
Business and Other Taxes	$12.8		Administration	$1.5	
Sales Tax/Fees	$4		Parks	$1	
			Utilities	$6.5	
			Housing Support	$1.5	
			Roads	$4.4	
			Hospitals	$3	
			Interest on Debt*	$1.6*	$1.6*
			All Other Expenses	$12	
Totals	$59		**Totals**	$61	

*Note: Interest on debt and state/federal aid can't be changed.

What are the advantages and disadvantages of your alternatives?

_____

_____

_____

Summarize the reasons for your recommended budget and tax proposal:

_____

_____

Modify

Write your evaluation for each of the situations given on the previous page. Use a separate
sheet of paper.

CHAPTER 14 How can taxation meet the needs of government and the people?

Name: _____

Essay

How can taxation meet the needs of government and the people?

Benjamin Franklin once wrote that nothing is certain "except death and taxes." Taxes have never been popular in the United States. However, without taxes, we wouldn't have many of the goods and services we need in our society—such as highways, national defense, and public schools. Consider the following information:

- Taxes can be progressive, proportional (flat), or regressive. Federal income taxes are currently progressive, requiring those with higher incomes to pay a higher percentage in taxes. Most real estate taxes are proportional, using a single rate to determine taxes on properties with different values. Sales taxes are regressive, since poorer people pay a larger percentage of their income for sales taxes than richer people.

- There is constant debate at the federal, state, and local levels about whom should be taxed and by how much. People have conflicting views of what is a "fair" tax.

- Governments spend tax revenues to provide different services. Mandatory spending is required by law and cannot be changed without changing the law. At the federal level, about two-thirds of all spending goes to mandatory items, such as Social Security, Medicare, and Medicaid, and to pay off the national debt.

- About half of all federal discretionary spending goes to defense, while the other half is divided among education, law enforcement, environmental protection, and other areas.

- State and local taxes are collected to pay for services such as road repairs, firefighting, and police protection. Local taxes are also the main funding source for public schools.

What Do You Think?

What is your opinion? Write a response to the Essential Question, **How can taxation meet the needs of government and the people?** Consider the information above, the Guiding Questions in your textbook, and the activities you have completed in your Journal and at Economics Online, including the WebQuest. See page 183 for a rubric for writing an Essential Question essay.

Don't Forget

Your answer to this question will help you think about the Unit 6 Essential Question: **What is the proper role of government in the economy?**

Warmup

 How effective is fiscal policy as an economic tool?

A. The money the federal government collects in taxes and spends on goods and services has a significant effect on the economy. Think about each of the issues below and then complete the chart.

Issue	How does this affect you/others?	What do you think the government should do about this issue, and why?
The budget calls for more spending on interstate highways.	*An improved highway system might reduce everyone's transportation costs. . . .*	*Government should spend more on alternative transportation systems. . . .*
Half the workers at a local plant are laid off when a government contract ends.		
The media reports that the national debt is higher than it has ever been.		
A government college loan program reduces the available loan amounts and raises interest rates.		
You land a good job at a firm doing research for the National Institutes of Health.		
Prices for food and gasoline keep rising each week.		

B. Fiscal policy is the government's use of spending and taxes to influence the economy. How do you think the federal government's fiscal policy directly affects you? Explain.

_____

_____

Exploration

I. Creating the Federal Budget

➡ Find Out

A. Review each option below and consider its likely effect on the federal budget. Then write the number for each option on the budget "see-saw" below, based on whether it most likely would promote a budget deficit, a budget surplus, or a balanced budget.

1. Reduce taxes, increase spending.　　　3. Reduce taxes, reduce spending.

2. Increase taxes, increase spending.　　4. Increase taxes, reduce spending.

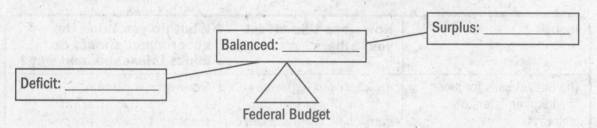

Surplus: _____

Balanced: _____

Deficit: _____

Federal Budget

B. The timeline below illustrates how long it generally takes to create a federal budget. Select two points on the timeline. At each point, list an event that might affect the budget process. Note how each one could affect the final budget. An example is given.

Federal Budget Timeline

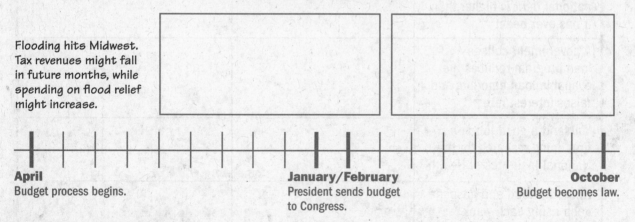

Flooding hits Midwest. Tax revenues might fall in future months, while spending on flood relief might increase.

April
Budget process begins.

January/February
President sends budget to Congress.

October
Budget becomes law.

👤 What Do You Think?

C. In the federal budget, the Office of Management and Budget (OMB) usually gives each federal agency less money than it requested. Why do you think the OMB does this?

_____

_____

II. Using Fiscal Policy

➔ Find Out

A. Fill in the top set of boxes below to describe the possible short-term effects of different fiscal policies. Then, fill in the remaining boxes to describe the possible long-term effects

Slowing Economy: Short-Term Effects

Government taxes _cut_ and spending _____

Economic production _____

Employment _____

Short-term results: _____

Rapidly Growing Economy: Short-Term Effects

Government taxes _rise_ and spending _____

Economic production _____

Employment _____

Short-term results: _inflation prevented_ _____

Long-Term Effects

Employment costs _rise_ and wages _____

Prices _____ as consumer spending _____

Long-term results: _____

Long-Term Effects

Employment costs _____ and wages _____

Prices _____ as consumer spending _____

Long-term results: _____

👤 What Do You Think?

B. Suppose that you're a U.S. Senator for your state. It's your turn to vote on a new law that requires the federal budget to be balanced each year. How do you vote, and why?

_____

_____

III. Stabilizing the Economy

➡ Find Out

A. Explain how the automatic stabilizers of federal taxes and government transfer payments work to decrease consumer spending in periods of high national income.

_____

_____

B. Fill in the chart below to show the differences in classical, demand-side, and supply-side economic theories about responding to an economic crisis such as a recession.

Classical Economics	Demand-side Economics	Supply-side Economics
Government should take these steps: _____ _____ _____ _____	Government should take these steps: _____ _____ _____ _____	Government should take these steps: _____ _____ _____ _____
The economy will improve because: _____ _____ _____ _____	The economy will improve because: _____ _____ _____ _____	The economy will improve because: _____ _____ _____ _____

👤 What Do You Think?

C. Which theory do you think would work best in responding to a recession, and why?

_____

_____

IV. Budget Deficits and the National Debt

➔ Find Out

A. Suppose that your parents give you a U.S. Savings Bond for your birthday. In five years, your bond will be worth $1,000. In this situation, who is actually borrowing the money and paying interest on the debt? What might the borrower do with this money?

_____

_____

B. Review the graph and answer the questions below.

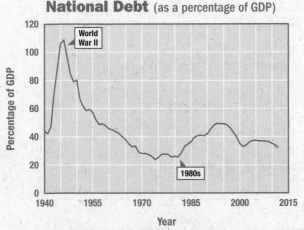

National Debt (as a percentage of GDP)

Note: Figures for the years 2007–2012 are projected.
SOURCE: The Executive Office of the President of the United States, The Office of Management and Budget.

What two government actions under President Reagan during the 1980s caused the national debt as a percentage of GDP to rise?

_____

_____

What factors have influenced the national debt since 2000?

_____

_____

C. In 2000, the federal government paid about $250 billion in interest on the national debt. How does that amount compare to other years? Research interest payments on the national debt, using online and print resources. List the interest paid on the national debt for at least two years (other than 2000). Why do you think the interest payments differ?

_____

_____

👤 What Do You Think?

D. Some economists and elected officials feel that the size of the current national debt is a significant problem, while others do not. How much of a problem do you think it is? How do you think it might affect your future?

_____

_____

_____

Essential Question Activity

 ## How effective is fiscal policy as an economic tool?

Activity

Complete this activity to answer the Essential Question.

Work in small groups, with each group researching the administrations of John F. Kennedy to the current President. Use the worksheet on the next page to gather the following information:

A. Identify the President by political party and years in office.

B. Identify the main economic goals and challenges under that administration.

C. Describe any tax and spending changes that grew out of the administration's fiscal policy.

D. Evaluate how successful that administration was at meeting its goals.

Modify

After your group has filled out its worksheet, make enough copies to distribute to the other groups in the class.

A. Each group will take the worksheets and evaluate which President they think had the most successful fiscal policy. Place the sheets in order from most effective policy to least effective.

B. The class will share and compare their conclusions.

C. As a class, make a generalization about the use of fiscal policy by Presidents since 1960 to stabilize economic conditions, stimulate growth, or cool down an overheated economy.

President:	_____
Political party:	_____
Years in office:	_____
What were the main economic goals and challenges under this administration?	Main economic goals: _____ _____ Main economic challenges: _____ _____
How would you describe the tax and spending changes that grew out of this administration's fiscal policy?	Tax changes: _____ _____ Spending changes: _____ _____
How successful was this administration in meeting its goals? Evaluate its success.	Evaluation: _____ _____ _____ _____

List the three main sources you used to find the above information: _____

_____

_____

Modify

Which administration do you think was most effective? Least effective? Why?

_____

_____

Write a generalization about the use of fiscal policy by Presidents since 1960:

_____

_____

Essay

How effective is fiscal policy as an economic tool?

There is no doubt that the U.S. government, through taxing and spending, greatly influences the economy. For example, in the 1930s, the government increased spending to increase the demand for goods and services. Then, in the 1980s, it used tax cuts to increase the supply of goods and services. Today, the national debt is higher than it has ever been and economists debate what this fact means for the future. Consider the following issues:

- The federal budget involves over $2.5 trillion in taxes and about an equal amount of spending. Currently, it takes Congress and the President about 18 months to finalize the yearly budget. How do you think this budget process can be improved?

- Fiscal policy can take a long time to have an effect on the economy. Do you think that the effects of fiscal policy can take place sooner? If yes, how? If not, why not?

- Some economists believe that the best way to respond to a recession or a depression is for the government to increase spending. Do you agree? Why or why not?

- In the 1980s, President Reagan and government economists emphasized increasing the supply of goods, rather than the demand for them. They cut taxes, thinking that people would be motivated to work more, to increase production and supply. Do you think cutting taxes results in economic growth? Why or why not?

- When the government does not bring in enough revenue to pay for its spending, it has to borrow money. Should Congress and the President be required to reduce government borrowing? Why or why not?

👤 What Do You Think?

What is your opinion? Write a response to the Essential Question, **How effective is fiscal policy as an economic tool?** Consider the issues above, the Guiding Questions in your textbook, and the activities you have completed in your Journal and at Economics Online, including the WebQuest. See page 183 for a rubric for writing an Essential Question essay.

> ### Don't Forget
> Your answer to this question will help you think about the Unit 6 Essential Question: **What is the proper role of government in the economy?**

CHAPTER 16 The Federal Reserve and Monetary Policy

Warmup

How effective is monetary policy as an economic tool?

A. The economic decisions each person makes influences the economy as a whole—and influences what actions the government will take to help grow, or slow, the economy. Choose one answer that best reflects what you would do in each situation below. Then, complete the rest of the chart based on your answers.

Situation Suppose that . . .	What would you do?	How would your choice affect your finances?	How would your choice affect the economy?
You want to buy a new car for $15,000. Once, you were offered payments of $325 per month for 5 years. Now, your payments would be $570/ month for 3 years.	__ keep my old car __ buy a used car __ buy the new car __ other _____ _____		
A credit card company offers you a $1,000 credit line for a spring break vacation. The fine print says you will pay $1450 over 20 months if you pay the minimum payments.	__ refuse the offer __ accept the offer __ ask a parent for a loan __ other _____		
You want to borrow $1,000,000 to expand your business. At first, you planned to pay off the loan in 5 years, but a higher interest rate means it will now take you 10 years.	__ refuse the loan __ take the loan __ sell stock to raise the money __ other _____		
You are elderly and want to sell your house for $250,000. But sales are slow because interest rates are high.	__ lower price by 2% __ lower price by 5% __ don't sell house __ other _____		

B. List two questions you have about the Federal Reserve System's role in our economy:

1. _____

2. _____

CHAPTER 16 How effective is monetary policy as an economic tool?

Name: _____

Exploration

I. The Federal Reserve System

➔ Find Out

A. Go to www.federalreserve.gov/otherfrb.htm, click on your Federal Reserve District, review the information there, and fill in the left part of the chart below. Then, choose another district, review the information, and fill in the right part. Lastly, complete the center area of the chart.

Your district: _____	Both	Other district: _____
Areas of growth:	Similar areas of growth:	Areas of growth:
Areas of decline:	Similar areas of decline:	Areas of decline:
Future possibilities:	Similar future possibilities:	Future possibilities:

B. Explain how the structure of the Federal Reserve System (the Fed) prevents your district from acting in a way that might help your district, but hurt another district.

_____

_____

C. Note that the Fed is privately owned by its member banks. How does this structure help insure that the Fed will act in the best interests of the national economy?

_____

_____

👤 What Do You Think?

D. How do you think the Fed's monetary policy affects your community? Your family? You? Explain.

_____

_____

_____

CHAPTER 16 How effective is monetary policy as an economic tool?

Name: _____

II. The Fed at Work

→ Find Out

Suppose that many people want to withdraw their money from Third-Rate Bank all at once.

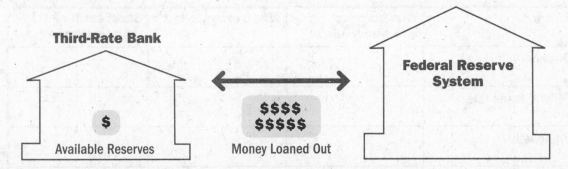

Third-Rate Bank

$

Available Reserves

$$$$
$$$$$

Money Loaned Out

Federal Reserve System

A. How do the Federal Reserve's banking regulations affect this situation?

_____

_____

B. What steps could the Fed take to keep this bank from failing?

_____

_____

👤 What Do You Think?

C. Suppose that when examiners from the Fed go to Third-Rate Bank, they find that the bank has been lending money to people who are considered poor credit risks. What actions do you think the examiners should recommend?

_____

_____

D. Do you think people who have accounts at Third-Rate Bank should be notified of the bank's risky loan practices? Why or why not?

_____

_____

E. How important do you think people's confidence in the banking system is to the overall economy? Explain.

_____

_____

CHAPTER 16 How effective is monetary policy as an economic tool?

Name: _____

III. Creating Money

→ Find Out

A. Fill in the chart below to identify the factors that help explain the differences among loan rates.

	Who borrows and who lends?	Who sets rate?	Short-term or long-term loan?
Discount rate			
Federal funds rate			
Prime rate			
Home mortgage rate			

B. The required reserve ratio (RRR) is the fraction of deposits that the Fed requires banks to keep in reserve. Fill in the boxes below to figure the difference in the total dollars created when the RRR is set at 9% and at 12%.

Bank loan of $1	Initial $ created	Amount loaned after RRR	Amount loaned after 2nd transaction	Total amount created for each $1	Total amount created for $1,000,000 in loans
RRR of 8%	$1	$.92			
RRR of 12%	$1	$.88			

C. Total bank loans that are outstanding for individuals and businesses equal trillions of dollars each year. Why does a small change in the RRR result in such a large difference in the total amount of money created?

_____

_____

👤 What Do You Think?

D. Suppose that you had a business loan for $10,000, which you agreed to pay over five years. The Fed suddenly changes the RRR from 10% to 13%. How might this change affect you? Why do you think the Fed seldom changes the RRR as a part of its monetary policy?

_____

_____

CHAPTER 16 How effective is monetary policy as
an economic tool?

Name: _____

IV. Adjusting the Money Supply Using the Open Market

→ Find Out

A. Fill in the boxes below to show how easy and tight monetary policies affect the supply of
money and the economy overall.

Easy Money Policy

| Fed decides the economy needs _more_ money available. | Fed tells NY trading desk to _____ a certain amount of bonds. | Private bond dealers _____ bonds. | Fed _____ money supply by _____. | Multiplier effect works to help economy _____. |

Tight Money Policy

| Fed decides the economy needs _____ money available. | Fed tells NY trading desk to _____ a certain amount of bonds. | Private bond dealers _____ bonds. | Fed _____ money supply by _____. | Multiplier effect works to help economy _____. |

B. The law of supply and demand influences interest rates for borrowing. Explain how the
Fed influences interest rates through its open market operations.

_____

_____

_____

👤 What Do You Think?

C. Most people are not aware of the Federal Open Market Committee (FOMC) acting to
affect the money supply. Do you think this lack of awareness makes a difference in how
the economy responds? Do you think that the FOMC's actions should be more widely
publicized? Why or why not?

_____

_____

_____

_____

CHAPTER 16 How effective is monetary policy as an economic tool?

Name: _____

V. Monetary Policy vs. Fiscal Policy

➡ Find Out

A. Suppose that you are an economist in 2015 who predicts a recession in 2016. Fill in the boxes below to identify the possible positive and negative effects of using either fiscal policy or monetary policy.

Fiscal Policy	What are the possible actions to take?	When would the actions take effect and why?	What are the possible positive effects?	What are the possible negative effects?
The government's use of spending and taxes to influence the economy	• Lower the income tax rate • •	• • •	• • •	• • •
Monetary Policy				
The decisions the Fed makes about money and banking	• Buy more bonds • •	• • •	• • •	• • •

👤 What Do You Think?

B. Based on your completed chart above, which policy do you think the Fed should take to head off the 2016 recession, and why?

_____

_____

C. If accurate economic predictions are so difficult to make, should economists even try to make any predictions? Why or why not?

_____

_____

D. Return to the two questions you wrote about the Fed in the Chapter 16 Warmup. Write brief answers to your questions on another sheet of paper. If you have other questions, look for the answers in your library or on the Internet.

CHAPTER 16 How effective is monetary policy as an economic tool?

Name: _____

Essential Question Activity

How effective is monetary policy as an economic tool?

Activity

Complete this activity to answer the Essential Question.

Work in groups to gather information about the use of monetary policy to stimulate, downsize, or otherwise stabilize economies. Use the worksheet on the next page to gather the following information:

A. What steps did the United States take in order to prevent a recurrence of the Panic of 1907?

B. How did the Federal Reserve Board attempt to deal with the Great Depression? How successful was it?

C. How effective was the Federal Reserve Board in controlling the double-digit inflation of the late 1970s?

D. How did the Fed under Alan Greenspan attempt to steer the U.S. economy between recession and inflation? How effective was it?

E. What would happen to monetary policy if the United States abolished the Fed and returned to the gold standard?

Modify

You are members of the Federal Reserve Board who have just heard the above reports prepared by your research committees. Based on this history of government attempts to use monetary policy to control the economy, what advice would you give the Chairman of the Board for his testimony next week before the Senate Finance Committee?

A. Decide which is more likely today, recession or inflation.

B. Describe the political pressures on the Fed in determining monetary policy.

C. Come up with a plan for Fed action in the next four quarters.

D. Describe the pitfalls the Fed faces in creating monetary policy.

CHAPTER 16 How effective is monetary policy as an economic tool?

Name: _____

What was the date, general issue, and economic conditions at the time?	
What actions were taken, and why?	
What economic theory was used to guide the actions?	
How effective were these actions? Explain.	
Would you take the same actions today if the conditions were the same? Why or why not?	

Make additional copies of this worksheet as needed.

List the main sources you used to find the above information: _____

_____

_____

Modify

Respond to the questions given on the previous page. Use an additional sheet of paper, if necessary.

A. _____

B. _____

C. _____

D. _____

CHAPTER 16 How effective is monetary policy as an economic tool?

Name: _____

Essay

 ## How effective is monetary policy as an economic tool?

Like fiscal policy, monetary policy can be used to help stabilize the economy. Controlling the amount of money in the economy is one of the main tasks of the Federal Reserve System. Its decisions affect the interest rates that are paid on loans. "The cost of money" affects the prices of goods and services as well as all types of consumer and business investments. Consider the following issues:

- The Federal Reserve System is organized so that members can act independently of regional interests and political pressure. Some economists believe the Fed should have less power, while others suggest it should have more.

- The Fed could use bank regulations such as the required reserve ratio (RRR) to change the money supply. However, predictable regulations help stabilize the economy, so the Fed tends not to change the RRR because it might disrupt the banking system too much.

- The discount rate and the federal funds rate are short-term rates. The Fed sets these rates, and this affects how banks do business. However, the Fed does not use these rates as the main way to adjust the money supply.

- Like government spending, bank loans have a multiplier effect in creating money for the economy. The Fed generally controls the amount of money available for loans by buying or selling government securities on the open market. Many economists think that open market operations have many advantages over other economic tools. However, foreign countries currently buy a large percentage of government securities.

- The timing of actions that affect the money supply is crucial to their effectiveness. Monetary policy can be quickly implemented since it does not involve the political process. However, its effects may not be felt for many months or even years.

What Do You Think?

What is your opinion? Write a response to the Essential Question, **How effective is monetary policy as an economic tool?** Consider the issues above, the Guiding Questions in your textbook, and the activities you have completed in your Journal and at Economics Online, including the WebQuest. See page 183 for a rubric for writing an Essential Question essay.

 Don't Forget

Your answer to this question will help you think about the Unit 6 Essential Question: **What is the proper role of government in the economy?**

UNIT 6 Government and the Economy

Essay Warmup

People have different opinions about what the government's role in the economy should be. Analyze the opinions below and answer the questions that follow to help you focus your thinking on the Unit 6 Essential Question, **What is the proper role of government in the economy?**

> **Government spending should be significantly reduced. It has grown far too quickly in recent years, and most of the new spending is for purposes other than homeland security and national defense. Combined with rising entitlement costs associated with the looming retirement of the baby-boom generation, America is heading in the wrong direction. To avoid becoming an uncompetitive European-style welfare state like France or Germany, the United States must adopt a responsible fiscal policy based on smaller government.**
>
> —Daniel J. Mitchell, "The Impact of Government Spending on Economic Growth"

A. What danger does Daniel J. Mitchell see for the United States if it doesn't change its government spending policy? Do you agree or disagree with his viewpoint?

_____

_____

_____

> **Global competition, rising health costs, longer life spans with weaker pensions, less secure employment, and unprecedented inequalities of opportunity and wealth are calling for a much broader, more inclusive approach to helping all of us meet these challenges, one that taps government as well as market solutions. . . . We can wield the tools of government to build a more just society, one that preserves individualist values while ensuring that the prosperity we generate is equitably shared.**
>
> —Jared Bernstein, All Together Now: Common Sense for a Fair Economy

B. How well does Jared Bernstein think the government is responding to new economic challenges? Do you think the government is currently working effectively to build "a more just society?" Explain.

_____

_____

C. What does this cartoon suggest about taxes and government spending?

_____

_____

_____

D. Do you agree with this cartoonist's point of view? Why or why not?

_____

_____

_____

What Do You Think?

Choose one of the documents above and explain how it helps you answer the Unit 6
Essential Question, **What is the proper role of government in the economy?**

_____

_____

_____

_____

_____

_____

_____

_____

_____

_____

UNIT 6 Government and the Economy

Essay

 What is the proper role of government in the economy?

Write an essay that responds to the Unit 6 Essential Question. Use your answers to the Essential Question warmup on the previous pages, your answers to the chapter Essential Questions, and what you have learned in this unit. Keep in mind that your essay should reflect your thoughtful and well-supported personal point of view. Filling in the chart below will help you structure your essay. Go to page 183 for a rubric for writing an Essential Question essay.

Thesis Statement: _____

_____

Body Paragraph 1	Body Paragraph 2	Body Paragraph 3
Main Idea _____ _____ _____ _____	Main Idea _____ _____ _____ _____	Main Idea _____ _____ _____ _____
Supporting Details 1. _____ _____ _____ 2. _____ _____ _____ 3. _____ _____ _____	Supporting Details 1. _____ _____ _____ 2. _____ _____ _____ 3. _____ _____ _____	Supporting Details 1. _____ _____ _____ 2. _____ _____ _____ 3. _____ _____ _____

Conclusion: _____

_____

Unit 7 The Global Economy

 Essential Question

How might scarcity divide our world or bring it together?

Chapter 17 Essential Question

Should free trade be encouraged?

Chapter 18 Essential Question

Do the benefits of economic development outweigh the costs?

UNIT 7 The Global Economy

Warmup

 ## How might scarcity divide our world or bring it together?

Economic development, largely fueled by international trade, is significantly improving the lives of millions of people around the world. At the same time, it is causing environmental damage, food shortages, and violent conflicts. In Unit 7, you will study how the global economy works and explore responses to the Unit Essential Question.

International trade aids development, but there are trade-offs, as this photo shows.

Study this bar graph, based on statistics from the United Nations. Note that per capita means "per person" and GDP means "gross domestic product," which you learned about in Chapter 12.

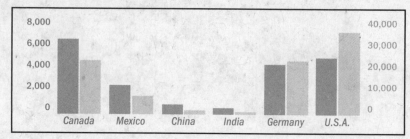

kilograms of energy used per capita

GDP per capita (U.S. dollars)

Canada Mexico China India Germany U.S.A.

A. Do you think there is a relationship between energy use and wealth (as measured by GDP)? Explain.

_____

_____

B. Should Mexico, China, and India try to increase their use of energy to increase their wealth? Why or why not?

_____

_____

C. Since energy resources are scarce, how could the United States use traditional resources more efficiently, or develop new resources, and still achieve its economic goals?

_____

_____

CHAPTER **17** **International Trade**

Warmup

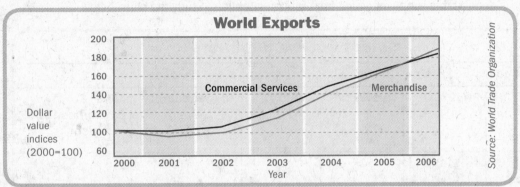

Should free trade be encouraged?

World Exports

Source: World Trade Organization

Dollar value indices (2000=100)

Commercial Services   Merchandise

Year: 2000 2001 2002 2003 2004 2005 2006

A. As you can tell from the graph above, free trade has greatly increased in recent years. (Free trade involves lowering or eliminating barriers to international trade.) In your opinion, has the rise in free trade resulted in positive or negative effects, or both? Next to each item, mark **+** if you think the effect has been positive, **–** if you think it has been negative, or **±** if you think it has been both (or had no effect).

___ U.S. consumers	___ foreign consumers	___ your family
___ U.S. workers	___ foreign workers	___ global peace
___ U.S. economy	___ global economy	___ global environment

B. Choose two items above and explain why you rated each one as you did. Provide at least one reason or example for each item.

_____

_____

_____

C. Do you think increasing free trade in the future would help or hurt the United States? Why?

_____

_____

D. How has increased free trade affected you or your family in recent years?

_____

_____

Exploration

I. The Need for Trade

👤 What Do You Think?

Suppose you plan to start a coffee shop. Since the United States doesn't grow much coffee, you need to find a dependable supply of coffee from foreign suppliers. Study the chart below.

Select Coffee Suppliers					
Scale: 1=poor 2=fair 3=good 4=very good 5=great					
Brand	Price/lb.	Variety	Quality	Dependability	Labor & Environmental Practices
Java Beans	$1.00	3	2	3	3
Kenya Flavors	$1.50	2	3	4	3
Costa Rica Blends	$2.00	2	4	3	5

A. Which coffee supplier would you use, and why?

_____

_____

B. Suppose severe weather hurts coffee crops in Kenya and in Costa Rica, doubling each of their prices. Which coffee supplier would you use now, and why?

_____

_____

C. As a coffee shop owner, which of the following is more important to you—a foreign supplier's prices or its environmental and labor practices—and why?

_____

_____

D. Should it matter to you that lower prices for you may mean poorer labor and environmental practices in a foreign country? Why or why not?

_____

_____

II. Who Has the Advantage?

→ Find Out

Compare the first two factories in the chart below. U.S. Factory #1 has an absolute advantage, being able to produce more of both types of cards than U.S Factory #2. However, U.S. Factory #2 has a comparative advantage over U.S. Factory #1.

	Collectible Cards (boxes per hour)	Greeting Cards (boxes per hour)	Opportunity Cost of 1 Box of Collectible Cards	Opportunity Cost of 1 Box of Greeting Cards
U.S. Factory #1	10	4	0.4 boxes of greeting cards	2.5 boxes of collectible cards
U.S. Factory #2	6	3	0.5 boxes of greeting cards	2.0 boxes of collectible cards
World Factory			____ boxes of greeting cards	____ boxes of collectible cards

A. Explain why U.S. Factory #2 has a comparative advantage over U.S. Factory #1.

_____

_____

B. Now suppose an overseas entrepreneur starts World Factory to compete with the two U.S. factories. Complete the chart above, using these numbers for World Factory:

5 = Collectible Cards (boxes per hour)   1 = Greeting Cards (boxes per hour)

👤 What Do You Think?

C. Which type of card do you think World Factory should produce? Why?

_____

_____

D. Suppose that you are the owner of U.S. Factory #1. What would you do to compete more effectively with the other two factories? For example, would you try to reduce costs? Improve quality? Produce something other than cards? Explain your decision.

_____

III. Free Trade or Protectionism?

➡ Find Out

A. What are some of the "pros and cons" of free trade? What are some of the "pros and cons" of protectionism, or the use of trade barriers? Complete the concept webs below with your responses.

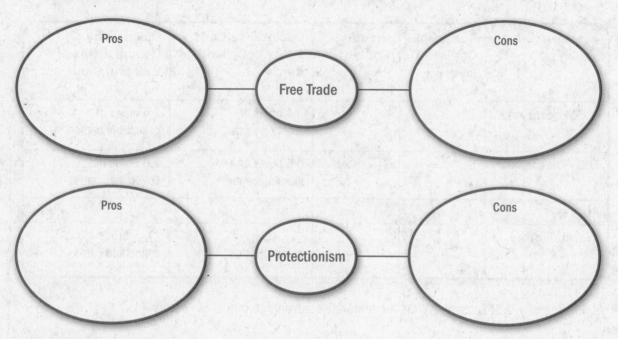

👤 What Do You Think?

B. In the webs, circle what you think is the most important "pro" in favor of free trade and the most important "pro" in favor of protectionism. Explain your choices.

_____

_____

C. Underline what you think is the most important "con" of free trade and the most important "con" of protectionism. Explain your choices.

_____

_____

D. In general, which position do you tend to favor: free trade or protectionism? Give at least two reasons to support your position.

_____

_____

Name: _____

IV. Balancing Trade and Payments

→ Find Out

A positive trade balance, or trade surplus, is when a country exports more goods and services than it imports. A negative trade balance, or trade deficit, is when a country imports more than it exports. Analyze the chart below to answer the questions that follow.

Selected Countries: Exports/Imports, 2006 (in $ billions)

Country	Services Exported	Services Imported	Goods Exported	Goods Imported
___ Brazil	$18	$27	$138	$96
___ Canada	$58	$72	$390	$358
___ China	$91	$100	$969	$792
___ Germany	$169	$219	$1112	$909
___ India	$74	$64	$120	$175
___ Japan	$123	$144	$650	$580
___ Mexico	$17	$23	$250	$268
___ South Africa	$12	$14	$58	$77
___ United Kingdom	$228	$172	$448	$619
___ United States	$389	$308	$1038	$1919

Source: World Trade Organization

A. Place a * next to the countries that had a trade surplus in services. Place a ** next to the countries that had a trade surplus in goods. Place a # next to the countries that had trade deficits for both goods and services.

B. Which country had the greatest trade surplus in services? _____

Which country had the greatest trade surplus in goods? _____

Which country had the greatest trade deficit in services? _____

Which country had the greatest trade deficit in goods? _____

👤 What Do You Think?

C. No country had a trade surplus for both goods and services. Why do you think this was so?

_____

_____

D. What do you think the U.S. government could do to reduce the U.S. trade deficit in goods? Explain your response.

_____

_____

Essential Question Activity

 Should free trade be encouraged?

Activity

Complete this activity to answer the Essential Question.

Your class will form six groups. One group will represent members of a U.S. Senate committee holding a hearing on a free-trade agreement with China being debated in Congress. Each of the other groups will represent one of the following:

· economists at the World Trade Organization   · an American consumer interest group

· an American car manufacturer   · the American Federation of Labor

· an organization of environmentalists

The senators should prepare their questions. The other groups should develop positions for or against the agreement. Using the worksheet on the next page, gather the following information:

A. What effects do the speakers think the agreement will have on the people or businesses they represent?

B. What effects do the groups think the agreement will have on the people of each senator's state?

C. What effects do the groups think the agreement will have on the country as a whole?

Modify

Congress sometimes insists on additions to agreements with other nations. Senators should explore these issues with each group. Then, they should announce:

A. What added provisions, if any, they would support and why.

B. Whether they will vote for or against the agreement.

A. Effects on people or businesses your group represents	B. Effects on people in senators' states	C. Effects on country as a whole
Possible Positive Effects:	**Possible Positive Effects:**	**Possible Positive Effects:**
• _____ _____ • _____ _____ • _____ _____ • _____ _____	• _____ _____ • _____ _____ • _____ _____ • _____ _____	• _____ _____ • _____ _____ • _____ _____ • _____ _____
Possible Negative Effects:	**Possible Negative Effects:**	**Possible Negative Effects:**
• _____ _____ • _____ _____ • _____ _____ • _____ _____	• _____ _____ • _____ _____ • _____ _____ • _____ _____	• _____ _____ • _____ _____ • _____ _____ • _____ _____

Modify

Respond to situation A, given on the previous page.

_____

_____

Respond to situation B, given on the previous page.

_____

_____

Essay

Should free trade be encouraged?

For individuals and businesses, free trade presents both challenges and opportunities. For example, it can create new jobs, but it can also result in job losses in certain fields. How does a country decide whether to engage in free trade, protectionism, or a combination of both? Consider these statistics and questions:

- According to the U.S. Census Bureau, world population is expected to reach 7 billion in 2012. Will an increase in global trade help more people to earn a living?

- According to the World Bank, the world's output of goods and services rose 4.8% in 2006, compared to 2005. Much of this rise was a result of global trade. Will more trade result in greater world output in the future?

- According to the U.S. Commerce Department, exports from the United States to 18 countries in the Middle East and Africa grew 22% from 2006 to 2007. What might happen in the future if these countries added trade barriers against U.S. exports?

- Based on U.S. Commerce Department statistics, the United States had a trade imbalance of about –$800 billion in 2007. Should our government impose more trade barriers?

- Based on U.S. Commerce Department statistics, the United States had its biggest trade imbalance with China, of about –$260 billion in 2007. Should our government impose more trade barriers on China?

What Do You Think?

What is your opinion? Write a response to the Essential Question, **Should free trade be encouraged?** Consider the items above, the Guiding Questions in your textbook, and the activities you have completed in your Journal and at Economics Online, including the WebQuest. See page 183 for a rubric for writing an Essential Question essay.

Don't Forget

Your answer to this question will help you think about the Unit 7 Essential Question: **How might scarcity divide our world or bring it together?**

18 Development and Globalization

Warmup

Do the benefits of economic development outweigh the costs?

A. Think about how you are affected by globalization, the interconnection of people and organizations around the world. Now think about how globalization affects other people. Then complete the chart below with examples from your experiences.

How globalization affects my life	How globalization affects the United States
How globalization affects my city/town	How globalization affects the world

EFFECTS OF GLOBALIZATION

B. In your opinion, what is the greatest effect of globalization today? Explain.

_____

_____

C. Economic development and globalization are closely linked in today's world. In your opinion, how important is globalization to future development? Use the scale below to rate its importance.

Low ◄ [ ][ ][ ][ ][ ][ ][ ][ ][ ] ► **High**

D. Provide at least two reasons to support your rating.

_____

_____

CHAPTER 18 Do the benefits of economic development outweigh the costs?

Name: _____

Exploration

I. Taking a Closer Look at Development

⇨ Find Out

A. Development is how a country improves the economic, political, and social well-being of its people. How do developed nations compare to less developed nations in each of these three areas? Complete the chart.

	Characteristics of Developed Nations	Characteristics of Less Developed Nations
Economics	Example: high per capita GDP	
Politics		Example: tend to have more central planning
Social Well-Being	Example: high literacy rate	

B. Use your completed chart to summarize the major differences between the United States and less developed countries.

_____

_____

_____

👤 What Do You Think?

C. Although the United States is a developed nation, its people have less leisure time—free time—than people in many other countries. Are there any characteristics not listed on your chart that you think economists should consider when evaluating a country's level of development? Explain.

_____

_____

CHAPTER 18 Do the benefits of economic development outweigh the costs?

Name: _____

II. Overcoming Obstacles to Development

→ Find Out

How a country uses its resources is critical to its level of development. Using the factors of production efficiently can fuel economic growth. However, using them inefficiently hurts development. Analyze development in these three hypothetical countries.

Oil Kingdom
· oil runs out in 2020
· exports more than imports
· little farmland; scarce water resources
· per capita income is $3,000/person
· literacy rate: males 60%; females 25%

Farmland Nation
· few energy resources
· imports more than exports
· productive rice farms; flooding a yearly risk
· per capita income is $1,000/person
· literacy rate: males 30%; females 30%

Tourist Republic
· few energy resources
· imports more than exports
· scenic beaches; few farms; scarce water resources
· per capita income is $1,500/person
· literacy rate: males 75%; females 70%

A. What is the biggest challenge facing each country, and why?

Oil Kingdom _____

_____

Farmland Nation _____

_____

Tourist Republic _____

_____

👤 What Do You Think?

B. Choose one of the hypothetical countries above. Based on the information in the chart, outline a three-step plan for how you think it could improve its economic development.

Step 1 _____

Step 2 _____

Step 3 _____

C. Many people around the world are subsistence farmers, barely able to feed themselves and their families. What do you think a country could do to improve its farm production?

_____

_____

CHAPTER 18 Do the benefits of economic development
outweigh the costs?

Name: _____

III. Moving to a Market Economy

➡ Find Out

A. The transition from a centrally planned economy to a free market economy has been
a difficult process for many countries. Complete the diagram below to describe this
process. Some of the information has been provided for you.

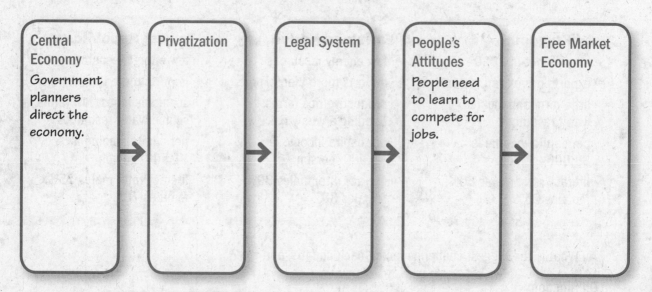

Central Economy	Privatization	Legal System	People's Attitudes	Free Market Economy
Government planners direct the economy.			People need to learn to compete for jobs.	

B. Which country has been more successful in its recent development—Russia, China, or
India? Provide supporting details for your opinion.

_____

_____

_____

C. Many countries in Africa and Latin America face challenges in their economic transitions.
What lessons might they learn from the experiences of Russia, China, and India? Explain.

_____

_____

_____

👤 What Do You Think?

D. Suppose that you were an entrepreneur, starting a business in a less developed country. Describe
what characteristics you would look for in the country where you would locate your business.

_____

_____

CHAPTER 18 Do the benefits of economic development outweigh the costs?

Name: _____

IV. Understanding the Impact of Globalization

→ Find Out

A. A car built in the United States may have parts made in many other countries. Research three products that you or your family uses, which are made or assembled in the United States, to find out where their parts or materials are made. (You can review product labels in stores or do Internet research.) Then, complete the chart below.

	Describe the product (company, style, and so on):	List the foreign parts/materials and country they were made in:
Product #1 _____		
Product #2 _____		
Product #3 _____		

● What Do You Think?

B. Do you think multinational companies play a negative or a positive role in globalization today? Explain.

_____

_____

C. Suppose you were a government official in a less developed country. Would you work to welcome—or to restrict—multinational companies in your country? Write a few sentences to persuade those who disagree with you to change their position.

_____

_____

_____

D. Predict the impact of globalization on your life ten years from today.

_____

_____

CHAPTER 18 Do the benefits of economic development outweigh the costs?

Name: _____

V. Meeting the Challenges of Globalization

→ Find Out

A. People have always argued about whether globalization offers more benefits than drawbacks. Does globalization help to solve the world's problems or does it only create more problems? Might it do both? Complete the chart below.

Issue of Globalization	What problem(s) does it help solve?	What problem(s) does it help create?
Interconnected Financial Markets	It makes stock trading easier, faster; it provides more choices for investors.	Trading in currency can hurt a country's economy if sales of its currency increase.
Multinational Companies		
Jobs		
Population		
Environment		
Resources		

👤 What Do You Think?

B. Do you think that globalization is a positive development? Why or why not?

_____

_____

_____

C. In your opinion, what could you do now to help the United States meet the challenges of globalization in terms of the world's scarce resources?

_____

_____

_____

CHAPTER 18 Do the benefits of economic development
outweigh the costs?

Name: _____

Essential Question Activity

Do the benefits of economic development outweigh the costs?

Activity

Complete this activity to answer the Essential Question.

Your class will form ten groups. Each group will take the part of a panel of officials at the International Monetary Fund, investigating economic conditions in a different LDC (less developed country). Use the library or Internet resources to find basic social, economic, and political information about your country. Using the worksheet on the next page, gather the following information:

A. What are the current social and economic conditions in the nation?

B. What resources or economic advantages does the nation have?

C. What economic problems does the nation face?

D. What is the nation's political system, and how stable is it?

Modify

Based on the information that was gathered, members of each group should meet together to create a development plan for the nation they are studying. The development plan should address the following issues:

A. What new or existing goods or services should be produced and sold? Why?

B. How should the nation obtain needed development funds?

C. What social or political changes will be needed for this program to succeed?

D. What social and economic benefits will result from this investment?

E. What potential negative effects might result from this development program? How can they be prevented?

With your group, prepare to present your conclusions to the rest of the class.

CHAPTER 18 Do the benefits of economic development outweigh the costs?

Name: _____

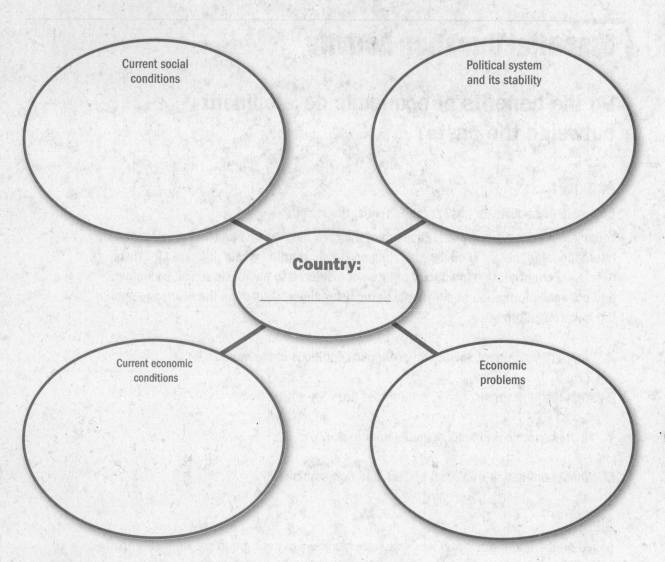

Modify

Respond to situation A or B, given on the previous page.

_____

_____

Respond to situation C or D, given on the previous page.

_____

_____

Respond to situation E, given on the previous page.

_____

_____

CHAPTER 18 Do the benefits of economic development
outweigh the costs?

Name: _____

Essay

Do the benefits of economic development outweigh the costs?

People have long debated the pros and cons of development and globalization. We
still debate these issues today—and will likely continue to do so. Are development and
globalization uncontrollable forces? Or can people around the world steer development
and globalization in positive directions? Consider these situations:

- Your home town's only printing plant is about to close, resulting in the loss
  of 90 jobs. The owner blames foreign competition. Suppose that you are an
  entrepreneur. Would you try to save the plant by buying it? Why or why not?

- The value of the dollar drops by 5% against both the Euro and the Japanese yen.
  Who benefits and who loses? Why?

- Severe weather destroys rice crops in several less developed countries. The result:
  the price of rice skyrockets and millions risk starvation. What should the U.S.
  government do, and why?

- Suppose that you're the owner of a small organic farm, raising corn and apples.
  Local grocery store managers won't buy from you, saying your prices are too
  high compared to the prices of non-organic crops from multinational agricultural
  companies. What would you do, and why?

- Your stock in a multinational company keeps increasing in value every year.
  However, you learn that its overseas factories pollute and pay very low wages.
  Would you keep your stock in that company? Why or why not?

What Do You Think?

What is your opinion? Write a response to the Essential Question, **Do the benefits of
economic development outweigh the costs?** Consider the topics above, the Guiding
Questions in your textbook, and the activities you have completed in your Journal and
at Economics Online, including the WebQuest. See page 183 for a rubric for writing an
Essential Question essay.

Don't Forget

Your answer to this question will help you think
about the Unit 7 Essential Question: **How might
scarcity divide our world or bring it together?**

UNIT 7 The Global Economy

Essay Warmup

Examine the following perspectives on the global economy. The questions that follow each perspective will help you focus your thinking on the Unit 7 Essential Question, **How might scarcity divide our world or bring it together?**

> Preliminary research indicates that scarcities of critical environmental resources—especially of cropland, freshwater, and forests—contribute to violence in many parts of the world. These environmental scarcities usually do not cause wars among countries, but they can generate severe social stresses within countries, helping to stimulate . . . ethnic clashes, and urban unrest. Such civil violence particularly affects developing societies because they are, in general, highly dependent on environmental resources and less able to buffer themselves from the social crises that environmental scarcities cause.
>
> —*Thomas F. Homer-Dixon,* Environment, Scarcity, and Violence

A. What does the author think is the main effect of scarcity of resources?

_____

_____

B. How might a scarcity of resources in one country affect a neighboring country?

_____

_____

> The potential exists to provide an adequate and sustainable supply of quality water for all, today and in the future. But there is no room for complacency. It is our common responsibility to take the challenge of today's global water crisis and address it in all of its aspects and dimensions.
>
> —*Jacques Diouf, UN Food and Agriculture Organization Director-General, March 2007*

C. Why do you think this speaker is focusing on the scarcity of water as a key challenge?

_____

_____

_____

_____

_____

arcadio/CAGLECARTOONS.COM/2008-IV.

D. What does this cartoon suggest about the global economy?

_____

_____

_____

E. What would you say in response to this cartoonist's point of view?

_____

_____

_____

What Do You Think?

Choose one of the documents above and explain how it helps you answer the Unit 7 Essential Question, **How might scarcity divide our world or bring it together?**

_____

_____

_____

_____

_____

_____

_____

UNIT 7 The Global Economy

Essay

 How might scarcity divide our world or bring it together?

Write an essay in response to the Unit 7 Essential Question. Use your answers to the Essential Question warmup on the previous pages, your answers to the chapter Essential Questions, and what you have learned in the unit. Keep in mind that your essay should reflect your thoughtful and well-supported personal point of view. Filling in the chart below will help you structure your essay. Go to page 183 for a rubric for writing an Essential Question essay.

Thesis Statement: _____

_____

Body Paragraph 1	Body Paragraph 2	Body Paragraph 3
Main Idea	**Main Idea**	**Main Idea**
_____ _____ _____ _____	_____ _____ _____ _____	_____ _____ _____ _____
Supporting Details	**Supporting Details**	**Supporting Details**
1. _____ _____	1. _____ _____	1. _____ _____
2. _____ _____	2. _____ _____	2. _____ _____
3. _____ _____	3. _____ _____	3. _____ _____

Conclusion: _____

_____

Rubric for Essential Question Essays

Criteria	Exceeds standard	Meets standard	Approaches standard	Does not meet standard
Thesis	Clear, well-developed thesis with clear connection to Essential Question	Clear and mostly developed thesis with clear connection to Essential Question	Somewhat clear thesis with limited connection to Essential Question	Unclear, or clear with little connection to Essential Question
Introduction	Clear, direct focus, highly interesting and engaging, provides excellent context for discussing Essential Question.	Focused and interesting, provides context for discussing Essential Question.	Somewhat focused and interesting, provides some limited context for discussing Essential Question.	Too broad, provides little context for discussing Essential Question. Uses throwaway phrases like "throughout history."
Supporting evidence and facts	Substantial facts and evidence	Sufficient facts and evidence	Uneven use of facts and evidence	Insufficient facts and evidence
Analysis	Effective, logical, sophisticated analysis; facts and evidence substantially enhance analysis; demonstrates keen insight into and understanding of Essential Question.	Effective, logical analysis; facts and evidence enhance analysis; demonstrates clear understanding of Essential Question.	General analysis only, and/or somewhat illogical or inconsistent. Facts and evidence somewhat enhance analysis; demonstrates basic understanding of Essential Question.	Limited analysis and/or illogical. Uses descriptive and storytelling format rather than analysis; demonstrates limited understanding of Essential Question.
Conclusion	Ties together main ideas to arrive at a logical and insightful conclusion that shows deep understanding of the Essential Question.	Ties together main ideas to arrive at a logical and insightful conclusion.	Demonstrates some understanding of the Essential Question and/or relies heavily on summary.	Demonstrates general and shallow understanding of the Essential Question or is summary only.
Organization and mechanics	Highly effective writing and organization; makes extremely few or no grammatical errors.	Effective writing and organization; makes few grammatical errors, which do not distract from the overall quality of the paper	Acceptable writing and organization. Some errors in spelling, grammar, punctuation, word choice, and capitalization. Includes repetition, fragments, conversational prose.	Weak organization and/or writing skills; many errors which detract from the quality of the paper

Photo and Art Credits

Text Credits